Building Smart Drones with ESP8266 and Arduino

Build exciting drones by leveraging the capabilities of Arduino and ESP8266

Syed Omar Faruk Towaha

BIRMINGHAM - MUMBAI

Building Smart Drones with ESP8266 and Arduino

Commissioning Editor: Vijin Boricha
Acquisition Editor: Namrata Patil
Content Development Editor: Trusha Shriyan
Technical Editor: Varsha Shivhare
Copy Editors: Laxmi Subramanian, Safis Editing
Project Coordinator: Kinjal Bari
Proofreader: Safis Editing
Indexer: Tejal Daruwale Soni
Graphics: Tania Dutta
Production Coordinator: Shantanu Zagade

First published: February 2018

Production reference: 1260218

Published by Packt Publishing Ltd.
Livery Place
35 Livery Street
Birmingham
B3 2PB, UK.

ISBN 978-1-78847-751-2

www.packtpub.com

`mapt.io`

Mapt is an online digital library that gives you full access to over 5,000 books and videos, as well as industry leading tools to help you plan your personal development and advance your career. For more information, please visit our website.

Why subscribe?

- Spend less time learning and more time coding with practical eBooks and Videos from over 4,000 industry professionals

- Improve your learning with Skill Plans built especially for you

- Get a free eBook or video every month

- Mapt is fully searchable

- Copy and paste, print, and bookmark content

PacktPub.com

Did you know that Packt offers eBook versions of every book published, with PDF and ePub files available? You can upgrade to the eBook version at `www.PacktPub.com` and as a print book customer, you are entitled to a discount on the eBook copy. Get in touch with us at `service@packtpub.com` for more details.

At `www.PacktPub.com`, you can also read a collection of free technical articles, sign up for a range of free newsletters, and receive exclusive discounts and offers on Packt books and eBooks.

Contributors

About the author

Syed Omar Faruk Towaha has degrees in physics and computer engineering. He is a technologist, tech speaker, and physics enthusiast from Shahjalal University of Science and Technology. He has a passion for programming, tech writing, and physics experiments. His recent publications include *Introduction to Rust Programming*, *Learning C for Arduino*, and *JavaScript Projects for Kids*. Over the last decade, he has worked on a number of projects related to physics, computer science, electronics, and medical science. He is currently working as the CTO of an IT company.

About the reviewer

Ersin Gonul is a senior design engineer at Turkish Aerospace Industries in Ankara, Turkey. He has worked as an R&D engineer for companies that develop unmanned aerial vehicles. He holds a bachelor's, as well as a master's, in electrical and electronics engineering from Selcuk University, Turkey, in 2003 and from Hacettepe University, Turkey, in 2011, respectively. His expertise is in helicopter autopilots and unmanned systems. He is passionate about aviation, rotary wing aircrafts, VTOLs, and their control systems; he also holds a Helicopter Private Pilot License (PPL-H).

Packt is searching for authors like you

If you're interested in becoming an author for Packt, please visit `authors.packtpub.com` and apply today. We have worked with thousands of developers and tech professionals, just like you, to help them share their insight with the global tech community. You can make a general application, apply for a specific hot topic that we are recruiting an author for, or submit your own idea.

Table of Contents

Preface

Books on technology become outdated as soon as the technology changes faster and tries to take a good shape. But something that will not become outdated is the idea and thinking of something outside the box. In this book, we have discussed building some smart drones. We used a number of modern technologies, including Arduino and ESP8266, but you need to know one thing before starting this book. This book will enlighten you about building drones using the latest technology. To be honest, this book is not for complete beginners. You need to have a good working knowledge of electronics and programming. You need to know about Arduino and Wi-Fi technologies. All of the chapters are designed for you to get the idea and build full-phase drones. But you might miss something that is untold there, which is a challenge for you to research and increase the thirst for the drone technology, but to build successful drones, all you need is a lot of motivation, as everything you want to include in your drone is already on the market, you just have to gather them, code them, and use them. I hope this book will help you to make your journey on the path of building smart drones easier. Who knows, someday you may create something that no one ever imagined. I will wait for your success and will be delighted to know if you make anything smarter.

Who this book is for

This book is for anyone who wants to build a drone, but he needs to be good at programming and electronics if he wants to build smart drones.

What this book covers

Chapter 1, *Things to Know Before You Build a Drone*, discusses all the basic ideas about drones, how you can identify them, what types of things are required to make drones, and explains a lot of preliminary ideas.

Chapter 2, *Assembling Your Drone*, helps you to start assembling our drone, install the modules to the drone, and get a very basic drone ready for flying. You'll also learn some aerodynamics regarding the flying of a drone. You'll learn some tricks to avoid crashing your drone in this chapter too.

Chapter 3, *Preparing Your Drone for Flying*, helps you to prepare your quadcopter for flight. We will learn how to calibrate some sensors and modes for the ArduPilot. In the end of the chapter, you'll learn how to configure the ESP8266 module and work with the mobile application.

Chapter 4, *Building a Follow Me Drone*, enables you to build a Follow Me drone and modify the control of the drone via some mobile applications. You'll also learn how to configure GPS with your ESP8266.

Chapter 5, *Building a Mission Control Drone*, teaches you how to make a mission control drone and perform a survey or deliver a package. You will also get an idea of how to implement some sensors to make the mission control drone more efficient.

Chapter 6, *Building a Drone to Take Selfies and Record Videos*, helps you build an octocopter and then use it to take selfies. You'll also use a customized gimbal and control it with the ESP8266 and mobile applications.

Chapter 7, *Building Prototype Drones – Gliding Drones*, teaches a number of things related to aerodynamics and designing a fixed wing drone. You'll learn how to use your ArduPilot for the glider at the end of the chapter. The physics behind flying will be explained in this chapter using simple mathematics.

Chapter 8, *Building Prototype Drones – Racing Drone*, shows how you can make a racing drone and get it ready for flying in a race. You'll also see how to tweak the obstacles using ESP8266 at the end of the chapter.

Chapter 9, *Maintaining and Troubleshooting Your Drone*, explains how to maintain your drone, and if your drone gets into any problems, how to troubleshoot them. In this chapter, you'll also learn some rules and regulations for flying drones.

To get the most out of this book

The drones you will build throughout this book will require a strong programming and electronics background. You will need to use Arduino IDE to upload the code to your ESP8266 and Arduino boards. For flashing the ESP8266, you will need to use the ESP flasher and the proper .bin files. A good working knowledge of C, C++, Python, and Lua will be required to play with the modules discussed in this book. You'll use Mission Planner, along with mobile applications such as Blynk, Tower, and DroidPlanner 2. If you know the AT commands for serial communication, it would be great.

Download the example code files

You can download the example code files for this book from your account at
www.packtpub.com. If you purchased this book elsewhere, you can visit
www.packtpub.com/support and register to have the files emailed directly to you.

You can download the code files by following these steps:

1. Log in or register at www.packtpub.com.
2. Select the **SUPPORT** tab.
3. Click on **Code Downloads & Errata**.
4. Enter the name of the book in the **Search** box and follow the onscreen
   instructions.

Once the file is downloaded, please make sure that you unzip or extract the folder using the
latest version of:

- WinRAR/7-Zip for Windows
- Zipeg/iZip/UnRarX for Mac
- 7-Zip/PeaZip for Linux

The code bundle for the book is also hosted on GitHub at https://github.com/
PacktPublishing/Building-Smart-Drones-with-ESP8266-and-Arduino. In case there's an
update to the code, it will be updated on the existing GitHub repository.

We also have other code bundles from our rich catalog of books and videos available at
https://github.com/PacktPublishing/. Check them out!

Download the color images

We also provide a PDF file that has color images of the screenshots/diagrams used in this
book. You can download it here: http://www.packtpub.com/sites/default/files/
downloads/BuildingSmartDroneswithESP8266andArduino_ColorImages.pdf.

Conventions used

There are a number of text conventions used throughout this book.

`CodeInText`: Indicates code words in text, database table names, folder names, filenames, file extensions, pathnames, dummy URLs, user input, and Twitter handles. Here is an example: "Mount the downloaded `WebStorm-10*.dmg` disk image file as another disk in your system."

A block of code is set as follows:

```
Blynk.begin(auth, ssid, pass); //This will start the Blynk with
proper credentials
pinMode(4, OUTPUT); //for trigger in D1
pinMode(5, INPUT); //for echo in D2
```

Bold: Indicates a new term, an important word, or words that you see onscreen. For example, words in menus or dialog boxes appear in the text like this. Here is an example: "Click on **New Project**, and name your project anything you want."

Warnings or important notes appear like this.

Tips and tricks appear like this.

Get in touch

Feedback from our readers is always welcome.

General feedback: Email `feedback@packtpub.com` and mention the book title in the subject of your message. If you have questions about any aspect of this book, please email us at `questions@packtpub.com`.

Errata: Although we have taken every care to ensure the accuracy of our content, mistakes do happen. If you have found a mistake in this book, we would be grateful if you would report this to us. Please visit www.packtpub.com/submit-errata, selecting your book, clicking on the Errata Submission Form link, and entering the details.

Piracy: If you come across any illegal copies of our works in any form on the Internet, we would be grateful if you would provide us with the location address or website name. Please contact us at copyright@packtpub.com with a link to the material.

If you are interested in becoming an author: If there is a topic that you have expertise in and you are interested in either writing or contributing to a book, please visit authors.packtpub.com.

Reviews

Please leave a review. Once you have read and used this book, why not leave a review on the site that you purchased it from? Potential readers can then see and use your unbiased opinion to make purchase decisions, we at Packt can understand what you think about our products, and our authors can see your feedback on their book. Thank you!

For more information about Packt, please visit packtpub.com.

Disclaimer

The information within this book is intended to be used only in an ethical manner. Do not use any information from the book if you do not have written permission from the owner of the equipment. If you perform illegal actions, you are likely to be arrested and prosecuted to the full extent of the law. Packt Publishing does not take any responsibility if you misuse any of the information contained within the book. The information herein must only be used while testing environments with proper written authorizations from appropriate persons responsible.

1

Things to Know Before You Build a Drone

Let me guess why you are reading this chapter—because you have some knowledge of Arduino and you are interested in building something awesome with it, which is a drone. Right? If yes, then this book is for you. Throughout this book, we will learn how to build a full-phase drone with the help of Arduino and other technologies. We will also build some prototype drones. If you don't have a basic idea about Arduino, I would recommend you read *Learning C for Arduino* before starting this book. In this book, we will learn how to build a drone from scratch and we will also modify the drone to serve our other purposes, such as Follow Me drones, mission-control drones, selfie drones, gliding drones, and racing drones. We will also learn how to maintain the drones and troubleshoot when needed.

In this chapter, we will cover the following topics:

- Definition and usages of drones
- Types of drones
- How we can identify or differentiate drones
- Introducing things needed to build a drone

If you feel enthusiastic about build your own drone, then come with me; let's start a journey together to build drones and have a lot of fun.

Drone

When you were a kid, did you have fun with paper planes? They were so much fun. So, what is a gliding drone? Well, before answering this, let me be clear that there are other types of drones, too. We will know all common types of drones soon, but before doing that, let's find out what a drone first. Drones are commonly known as **Unnamed Aerial Vehicles (UAV)**. A UAV is a flying thing without a human pilot on it. Here, by thing we mean the aircraft. For drones, there is the **Unnamed Aircraft System (UAS)**, which allows you to communicate with the physical drone and the controller on the ground. Drones are usually controlled by a human pilot, but they can also be autonomously controlled by the system integrated on the drone itself. So what the UAS does, is it communicates between the UAS and UAV. Simply, the system that communicates between the drone and the controller, which is done by the commands of a person from the ground control station, is known as the UAS. Drones are basically used for doing something where humans cannot go or carrying out a mission that is impossible for humans. Drones are used mainly by military men, scientific research, agriculture, surveillance, product delivery, aerial photography, recreations, traffic control, and of course, for terrorist attacks and smuggling drugs, which we will not be discussing in this book.

Types of drones

Drones can be categorized into the following six types based on their mission:

- **Combat**: Combat drones are used for attacking in the high-risk missions. They are also known as **Unnamed Combat Aerial Vehicles (UCAV)**. They carry missiles for the missions. Combat drones are much like planes. The following is a picture of a combat drone:

- **Logistics**: Logistics drones are used for delivering goods or cargo. There are a number of famous companies, such as Amazon and Domino's, which deliver goods and pizzas via drones. It is easier to ship cargo with drones when there is a lot of traffic on the streets, or the route is not easy to drive. The following diagram shows a logistic drone:

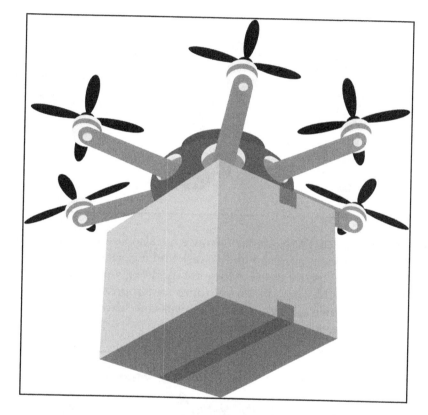

- **Civil**: Civil drones are for general usage, such as monitoring the agriculture fields, data collection, and aerial photography. The following picture is of an aerial photography drone:

- **Reconnaissance**: These kinds of drones are also known as mission-control drones. A drone is assigned to do a task and it does it automatically, and usually returns to the base by itself, so they are used to get information from the enemy on the battlefield. These kinds of drones are supposed to be small and easy to hide. The following diagram is a reconnaissance drone for your reference, they may vary depending on the usage:

- **Target and decoy**: These kinds of drones are like combat drones, but the difference is, the combat drone provides the attack capabilities for the high-risk mission and the target and decoy drones provide the ground and aerial gunnery with a target that simulates the missile or enemy aircrafts. You can look at the following figure to get an idea what a target and decoy drone looks like:

- **Research and development**: These types of drones are used for collecting data from the air. For example, some drones are used for collecting weather data or for providing internet.

We can also classify drones by their wing types. There are three types of drones depending on their wings or flying mechanism:

- **Fixed wing**: A fixed wing drone has a rigid wing. They look like airplanes. These types of drones have a very good battery life, as they use only one motor (or less than the multiwing). They can fly at a high altitude. They can carry more weight because they can float on air for the wings. There are also some disadvantages of fixed wing drones. They are expensive and require a good knowledge of aerodynamics. They break a lot and training is required to fly them. The launching of the drone is hard and the landing of these types of drones is difficult. The most important thing you should know about the fixed wing drones is they can only move forward. To change the directions to left or right, we need to create air pressure from the wing. We will build one fixed wing drone in this book. I hope you would like to fly one.

- **Single rotor**: Single rotor drones are simply like helicopter. They are strong and the propeller is designed in a way that it helps to both hover and change directions. Remember, the single rotor drones can only hover vertically in the air. They are good with battery power as they consume less power than a multirotor. The payload capacity of a single rotor is good. However, they are difficult to fly. Their wing or the propeller can be dangerous if it loosens.
- **Multirotor**: Multirotor drones are the most common among the drones. They are classified depending on the number of wings they have, such as tricopter (three propellers or rotors), quadcopter (four rotors), hexacopter (six rotors), and octocopter (eight rotors). The most common multirotor is the quadcopter. The multirotors are easy to control. They are good with payload delivery. They can take off and land vertically, almost anywhere. The flight is more stable than the single rotor and the fixed wing. One of the disadvantages of the multirotor is power consumption. As they have a number of motors, they consume a lot of power.

How can we differentiate between drones

We can also classify multirotor drones by their body structure. They can be known by the number of propellers used on them. Some drones have three propellers. They are called tricopters. If there are four propellers or rotors, they are called quadcopters. There are hexacopters and octacopters with six and eight propellers, respectively.

The gliding drones or fixed wings do not have a structure like copters. They look like the airplane. The shapes and sizes of the drones vary from purpose to purpose. If you need a spy drone, you will not make a big octacopter right? If you need to deliver a cargo to your friend's house, you can use a multirotor or a single rotor:

- The **Ready to Fly (RTF)** drones do not require any assembly of the parts after buying. You can fly them just after buying them. RTF drones are great for the beginners. They require no complex setup or programming knowledge.
- The **Bind N Fly (BNF)** drones do not come with a transmitter. This means, if you have bought a transmitter for your other drone, you can bind it with this type of drone and fly. The problem is that an old model of transmitter might not work with them and the BNF drones are for experienced flyers who have already flown drones with safety, and had the transmitter to test with other drones.

- The **Almost Ready to Fly** (ARF) drones come with everything needed to fly, but a few parts might be missing that might keep it from flying properly. Just kidding! They come with all the parts, but you have to assemble them together before flying. You might lose one or two things while assembling. So be careful if you buy ARF drones. I always lose screws or spare small parts of the drones while I assemble. From the name of these types of drones, you can imagine why they are called by this name. The ARF drones require a lot of patience to assemble and bind to fly. Just be calm while assembling. Don't throw away the user manuals like me. You might end up with either pocket screws or lack of screws or parts.

Drone frames

Basically, the drone frame is the most important to build a drone. It helps to mount the motors, battery, and other parts on it. If you want to build a copter or a glide, you first need to decide what frame you will buy or build. For example, if you choose a tricopter, your drone will be smaller, the number of motors will be three, the number of propellers will be three, the number of ESC will be three, and so on. If you choose a quadcopter it will require four of each of the earlier specifications. For the gliding drone, the number of parts will vary. So, choosing a frame is important as the target of making the drone depends on the body of the drone. And a drone's body skeleton is the frame. In this book, we will build a quadcopter, as it is a medium size drone and we can implement all the things we want on it.

If you want to buy the drone frame, there are lots of online shops who sell ready-made drone frames. Make sure you read the specification before buying the frames. While buying frames, always double check the motor mount and the other screw mountings. If you cannot mount your motors firmly, you will lose the stability of the drone in the air. About the aerodynamics of the drone flying, we will discuss them soon. The following figure shows a number of drone frames. All of them are pre-made and do not need any calculation to assemble.

You will be given a manual which is really easy to follow:

You should also choose a material which light but strong. My personal choice is carbon fiber. But if you want to save some money, you can buy strong plastic frames. You can also buy acrylic frames. When you buy the frame, you will get all the parts of the frame unassembled, as mentioned earlier.

The following picture shows how the frame will be shipped to you, if you buy from the online shop:

If you want to build your own frame, you will require a lot of calculations and knowledge about the materials. You need to focus on how the assembling will be done, if you build a frame by yourself. The thrust of the motor after mounting on the frame is really important. It will tell you whether your drone will float in the air or fall down or become imbalanced. To calculate the thrust of the motor, you can follow the equation that we will speak about next.

If P is the payload capacity of your drone (how much your drone can lift. I'll explain how you can find it), M is the number of motors, W is the weight of the drone itself, and H is the hover throttle % (will be explained later). Then, our thrust of the motors T will be as follows:

$$T = \frac{\frac{1}{H} \times (P + W)}{M}$$

The drone's payload capacity can be found with the following equation:

$$P = T \times M \times H - W$$

Remember to keep the frame balanced and the center of gravity remains in the hands of the drone.

Types of motors used for drones

There are a few types of motors that are use to build drones. But as the drone needs to be thrust in the air to float, we should use some powerful motors. The cheap, lightweight, small, and powerful motors used in drones are **Brushless DC motors (BLDC)**. For small drones, we do not use BLDC motors, but instead use small DC gear motors.

Several types of speed controllers

You cannot control the speed of motors of your drone unless you use speed controllers. They enable you to control the voltage and current of the motors and hence control the speed, which is the first priority to move the drone one place to another, after floating in the air. You need to increase and decrease the speed of motor(s) to move the drone forward, backward, left, or right.

The connection between the controller board of the drone and ESC and the battery/power distribution board will be shown in Chapter 2, *Assembling Your Drone:*

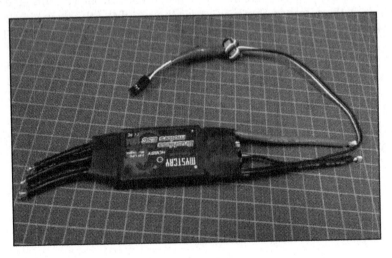

Refer to the following circuit diagram:

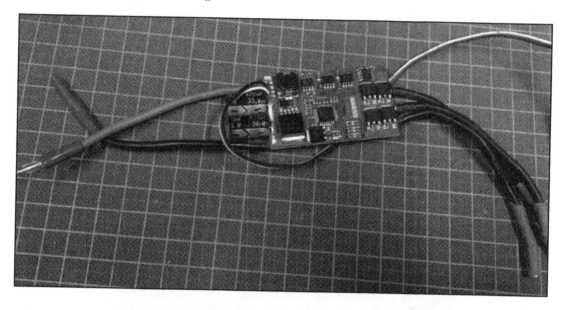

Flight control board

This is one of the most important things to control the drone from the ground. There are a number of flight control boards on the market. Some of them are open source and some of them are not. The following list has the most famous and top-rated flight controllers:

- KK 2.0
- CC3D
- Naze32
- KISS
- ArduPilot
- Vector
- 3DR Pixhawk
- DJI Nava M
- LUX flight controller
- DJI A3

In this book, we will use ArduPilot, as it is cheap and it is best for copters. It also covers our book title. The following picture of some flight controllers.

The ArduPilot is one of the best flight controllers for drones because of the following reasons:

- It has a free, open source autopilot framework supporting different types of drones
- It supports hundreds of 3D waypoints
- It allows you to do the autonomous take-off, landing, and camera control
- It has 4 MB onboard data-logging memory
- It has a built-in hardware fail-safe processor
- It has full mission scripting
- It is really simple to set up

The following picture is an ArduPilot:

We will discuss more about the ArduPilot later.

Radio transmitter and receiver

What the transmitter does is it sends a signal to the receiver. The receiver receives this signal and does according to the command from the transmitter. Since the drone floats in the sky, it needs to send signals to command the drone to move or do something. So we need the transmitter and receiver. There are lots of transmitters and receivers out there. The transmitter looks like a remote, which is controlled by the drone pilot and the receiver is connected to the flight controller. So, if the pilot gives commands from the transmitter to the drone, the drone receives it via the receiver and the flight controller processes the signal and does, as per the command of the pilot.

Battery

A drone is useless without a battery. All motors, flight controllers, radio, and processing require power. But it is not a wise decision to use the heavy battery to fly your drone because most of the energy will be spent on the thrust of a drone to fly. So, we need to choose light but powerful batteries. In a drone, we usually use lithium polymer batteries.

Choosing the right battery for the drone is one of the most critical things. Before choosing batteries for your drone, keep the following things in mind:

- Battery size and weight
- Battery discharge rate
- Battery capacity
- Battery voltage
- Battery connectors

You can easily calculate the continuous current output of the battery with the help of the following formula. If the current is I, battery capacity is C, and discharge rate is D, then the instantaneous current draw is $I = C \times D$. So always choose the highest capacity batteries, depending on the size and weight of the batteries. The LiPo, or Lithium Polymer battery has cells. Say you have three cells in your battery and each of them is 5,000 mAh and the discharge rating is 10 C.

So, the current draw is:

$$I = 5.0 \times 10 = 50\,A$$

Here, we converted mAh to Ah by dividing by 1,000. The following figure shows LiPo batteries for a drone:

Propellers

When you choose propellers for your drone, choose the lightest but strongest propellers. You also need to keep in mind that the propellers should be balanced on both sides. Most drone flight failure are due to a fault in the propellers. So choose carefully. Always choose the right size propellers. Follow the motor manuals to choose which size suits best.

The following figure shows different types of propellers:

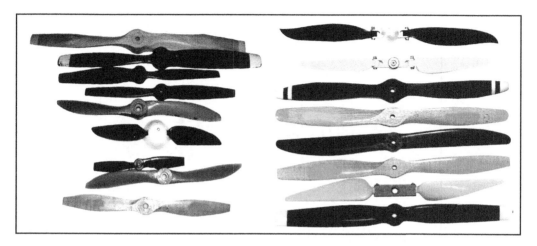

Battery adapters/chargers

Battery chargers are required to recharge your LiPo batteries. There are lots of LiPo chargers on the market. Always buy according to the manual of your battery. My suggestion is to buy a balance charger, which allows your battery to be charged with balance for all the cells.

Connectors

Connectors are the most important things for the power and other parts of the drone. If the connectors lose your drone, it might meet with an accident. So, buy connectors with special care according to the drone's power distribution system. You need to solder connectors properly with the batteries, ESCs, and other parts of the drone.

You need to buy bullet connectors, XT60, or T-plug connectors and use them where they suit:

Some modules to make the drone smarter

There are other modules to make the drone even smarter such as GPS, Wi-Fi module (for example, ESP8266), battery checkers, and range booster antennae, and so on.

Power distribution board

The power distribution board of the drone allows the components of the drone to get a proper current and draw a perfect voltage. We will have four ESCs; we can buy a power distribution board to deliver the proper current to all the ESCs. The following picture is a power distribution board of a drone:

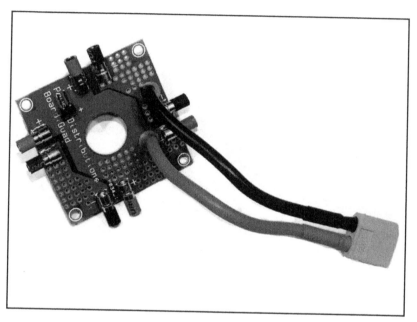

Summary

In this first chapter, we have learned what sort of things we will need to build a drone. We have learned a few tweaks for choosing batteries and frames. If you want to build your own drone, I hope you buy them before going to Chapter 2, *Assembling Your Drone,* because from this chapter onward, we will start assembling and flying our drone. Well, the full parts list will be given, so that you can buy the equipment in the proper quantities. So let's get started with Chapter 2, *Assembling Your Drone.*

2
Assembling Your Drone

In Chapter 1, *Things to Know Before You Build a Drone*, we were introduced to all the basic components of a drone. In this chapter, we will assemble our drone and make it ready for the next phase.

We will cover the following topics in this chapter:

- Assembling the frame
- Connecting the motor
- Connecting the ESC
- Connecting the ArduPilot
- Configuring the drone with the ArduPilot
- Aerodynamics needed for flying a drone
- Knowing security protocols for flying a drone
- Preventing the drone from crashing

To begin the process of building the quadcopter, we first need to assemble the frame. So, let's begin with our assembling.

Assembling the frame

The assembly of the drone frame requires a lot of patience and you are once again advised to follow the instruction manual when doing it for the first time. For reference, in this book, we will assemble a drone frame from HobbyKing (S500). Inside the box, you will get the items displayed in the following picture:

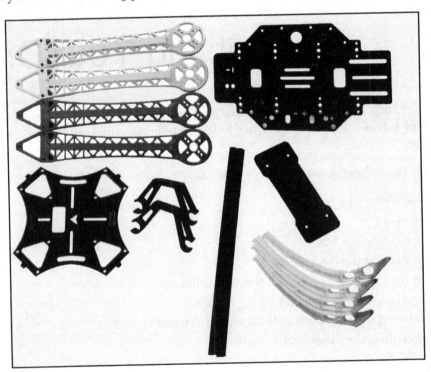

These items are listed here:

- Four frame arms (two blue and two black, if you buy the blue color)
- Four leg plates
- Two rods for the base mount
- One top plate
- One bottom plate for mounting the power lines
- And a lot of screws

Firstly, see the following figure and connect the parts as shown here:

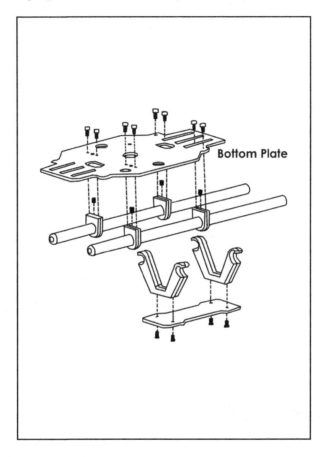

Use a proper screwdriver to tighten the screws. Do not keep any screws untightened or tilted.

Let's connect the motors now.

Connecting the motors

To connect the motors, you need to place the motor on the frame arm and attach the screws, as shown in the following figure, making sure you tighten the screws as much as you can, without breaking the frame arm:

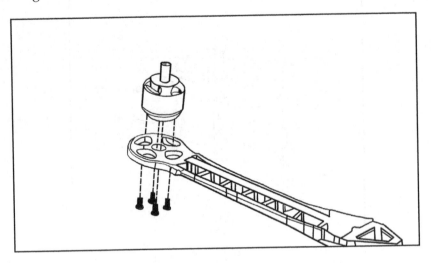

The BLDC has three wires coming out of the motor. We need to solder the bullet connector to them to be connected to the ESC. Now, connect the other three motors to the frame arms.

Connecting the ESC

Connecting the ESCs is one of the most important tasks in building a quadcopter or any other drone. You can buy four pieces of ESCs or a four-in-one ESC. I suggest you use a four-in-one ESC, which is lighter and easy to use.

If you use single a ESC, connect the wires of the motor to the ESC, as shown in the following figure. The connection of the motor and ESC do not matter because the wires are for changing the phase only:

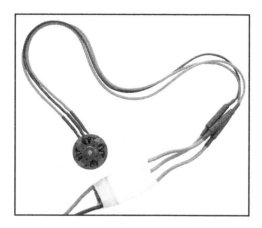

If you use a four-in-one ESC, the connections are also almost the same. I personally use Multirotor four-in-one ESCs from EMAX. Refer to the following figure to know how to connect the wires:

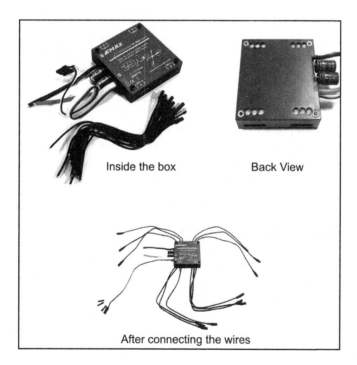

Inside the box   Back View

After connecting the wires

The *3 x 4 = 12* wires will be connected to the four BLDC motors. Let's look at the wire configuration. The single **ESC** has eight wires. Three wires go to the **BLDC** motor, two wires go to the power unit, the remaining three wires are for signal, ground, and power. If you configure the ESC with an Arduino, the diagram will be as follows:

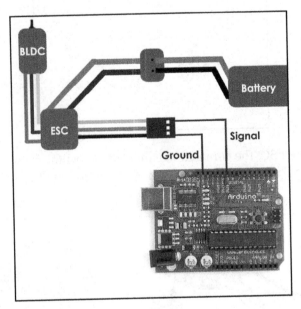

For connecting to the Arduino, we do not use the power of the ESC cable. The main wire is the signal cable. We use this to simulate the core of the motor to turn. If you want to use an Arduino as the main control board of your drone, then you need to connect all of your ESCs, as shown in the previous figure, choosing different signal pins.

Connecting the ArduPilot

Connecting the ArduPilot is one of the most important tasks for flying and controlling the drone. The ArduPilot is basically the brain of our drone. It enables the drone to control the movement, the camera, and the other sensors connected to it. We will connect a radio to our ArduPilot later, so that we can control the drone remotely.

Let's look at the ArduPilot first.

The ArduPilot has basically eight types of pins, as marked in the following diagram. Lets look at the what the uses of them are:

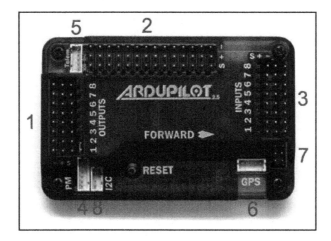

These pins are used to add the ESCs signal or output cables. Remember the three wires of the ESCs? They will be connected here. You can add up to eight ESCs in the ArduPilot. The rightmost pin of a row is used for the signal cable, the middle pin is for the power cable, and the leftmost pin is the ground pin. See the following diagram for a better idea:

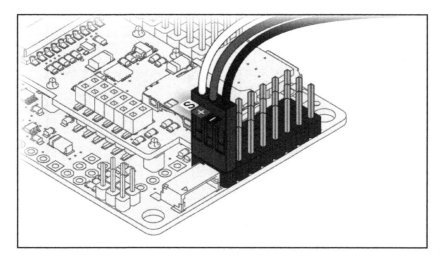

There are some specific rules in which orientation you should connect your ESCs output wired to the ArduPilot. As we are building a quadcopter, the opposite motor of a motor should rotate in the same direction (clockwise or anticlockwise). There are two kinds of quadcopters depending on the shape of the quad's hands. One is plus shaped and the other is cross shaped. The motors must be connected, as shown in the following figure:

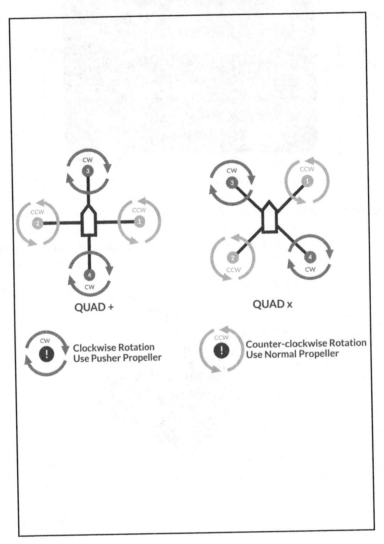

If you are unsure about which is the pusher propeller and which is the normal propeller, you may remember, pusher propellers rotate clockwise and normal propellers rotate anticlockwise. In the propellers, you may find **P** or **R** after size marks. P or R denotes that it is a pusher propeller, otherwise it is a normal propeller. See the following diagram for more clarification:

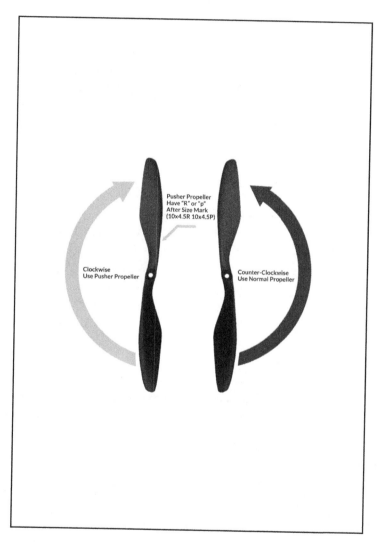

These pins are used for the analogue sensor pins of the drone (for example, sonar sensor, airspeed sensor, voltage or current sensor, and so on). We will learn more about the pins' uses in the coming chapters. Refer to the following diagram to know how the sonar sensor is connected to the ArduPilot:

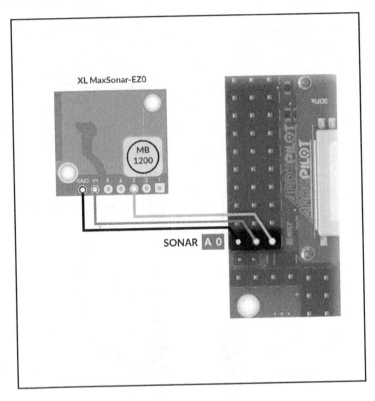

These pins are used for connecting the remote or radio or RC receiver to the ArduPilot. We will learn how to connect a radio to the ArduPilot in a while.

These pins are used for adding a common power module to the ArduPilot board. The common power module provides 5.37V and 2.25 Amp power supply. It allows the ArduPilot to work more accurately with a lot of sensors connected to it, such as the compass sensor. A small variation of the power will cause the direction to go wrong. If there is a small variation of power, the direction will be changed because of that, as it will trigger the compass inaccurately. So, using a common power module to these pins is needed if you want good accuracy of the measurements from the sensors connected to and built into the ArduPilot.

In these pins, a Bluetooth device or an RF transreceiver (having 900 MHz or 2.4 GHz frequencies) is connected, so that it can communicate to the ground control station. It can cover up to 50 m or the radius, depending upon the model of the Bluetooth device. Using these pins, we can easily connect our drone to the computer without any wire and download flight data without any wire. We will discuss more about these devices in the coming chapters.

The ArduPilot does not come with a **Global Positioning System** (**GPS**) sensor or GPS Receiver. So, we have to connect an external GPS sensor or GPS Receiver, so that your drone can do some complex things related to GPS (for example, position holding and waypoints navigations). If you want to make your drone fully autonomous, this port is needed. We will discuss more about this port in the coming chapters.

If you look closely, you can see that a jumper is there. If the jumper is connected, the board will use the internal compass; if not, then the board will use the external compass. It is not necessary to remove the jumper unless you buy an external compass, or the on-board compass is not good. The compass is used to define the direction of the drone while flying. So, this is important for a smart drone.

This is a multifunction MUX port (in network communication systems, MUX is the short form of multiplexing, it can send multiple signals at the same time to another device), which is used to connect to the computer via UART0, UART2, I2C, or OSD. If you do not alter anything, the default setting is OSD.

Connecting the radio

Connecting the radio to the ArduPilot is one of the easiest things. You can choose a short-range or long range radio. I would suggest you use the 3DR radio. It is easy to set up via the ArduPilot software and is easy to use. The radio will be directly connected to the ArduPilot and will send signals to the receiver connected to the PC. This is required when your drone is fully assembled and you need to calibrate the drone without any external wire connected to it. The radio will be connected via the Telem port.

Connecting the RC receiver and transmitter

The RC transmitter allows the drone pilot to control the drone wirelessly. It would be silly to fly a drone with a wire in the sky, so connecting the **Radio Controlled** (**RC**) transmitter is a must for a drone.

The RC transmitter sends signals and the receiver receives the signal. The RC transmitter is also known as the TX and the RC receiver is known as the RX. Before discussing about the RC receiver, let's know the transmitter first.

Basically, the transmitter is the remote controller of the drone. Before choosing a perfect transmitter, you need to consider a few things, such as the number of channels, the modes, and the frequency technology, and so on.

I would suggest you buy a good transmitter because this is the least thing that is destroyed while flying drones.

The number of channels gives you the ability to control how many individual actions you can control of the drone. Let's make it clear. Say a drone needs a few actions from the transmitter to be received by the receiver and enables the controller to execute the commands, such as the throttle, pitch, or yaw. These three actions will require three individual channels of the transmitter. To fly a drone properly, you need to choose at least a four-channel transmitter. Then you can easily control the throttle, roll, pitch, and yaw. We will know about them later. There are transmitters with a higher number of channels. There, you can also control the auxiliary channels.

The mode of the transmitter is also needed to be taken care of. There are usually four kinds of modes of a transmitter. They are known as numerically mode 1, mode 2, mode 3, and mode 4:

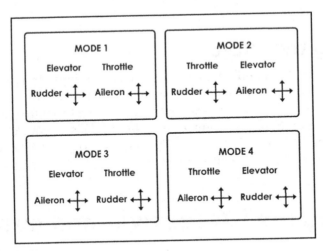

The previous diagram shows all four modes of the transmitter.

We see more details of the transmitter in `Chapter 3`, *Preparing Your Drone for Flying,* as it is a must to fly a drone.

Connecting the RC receiver to the ArduPilot is one of the hardest parts. Remember the input pins of the ArduPilot? We will connect our RC receiver there. Usually, the pin configuration is as follows:

- **Pin 1**: Roll/aileron
- **Pin 2**: Pitch/elevator
- **Pin 3**: Throttle
- **Pin 4**: Yaw/rudder
- **Pin 5**: Auxiliary channel 1 (for example, mode switch)
- **Pin 6**: Auxiliary channel 2

On the RC receiver, you will see the pin number/channel number. Just connect to the ArduPilot as you desire. Alternatively, you can follow the previous pin configuration to avoid complexity. See the following figure, if you need more clarification:

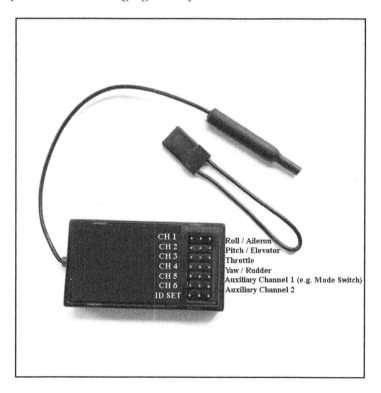

We will configure the transmitter as the setup of the RC receiver. I will be using a six-channel displayless transmitter from Fly Sky (model: FS-CT6B) throughout the book. You can use another transmitter, if you want. Both the transmitter and the receiver come with the single box, so you don't have to worry about the configuration now.

Connecting the battery

We are almost finished assembling our quadcopter. Now the last part is to connect the battery. As we are using, S500 frame, it comes with a board, where you can connect the battery by soldering the connectors to the board and later just plug the battery while flying the drone. You can use zipties to lock the battery under the body of the copter, as shown in the following figure:

To summarize the connections, let's recap. The BLDC motors will be connected to the four-in-one ESC (or four individual ESCs). The ESCs will be connected to the ArduPilot's output pins (only signal cables, 5V, and ground cables). The power cables of the ESC (or ESCs) will be directly connected to the battery (in our case, we have connected on the body plate first and later used connector pins to be connected to the battery.). The radio and the RC receiver will be connected to the Telem pins and input pins of the ArduPilot, respectively. That is it for a simple quadcopter.

Binding transmitter to the receiver

Binding is really important. Without proper binding, you cannot configure the drone's actions properly. You can bind your transmitter with at least the following things. Note that the binding process differs from the RC Receiver's model to model. The steps of the most common method is as follows:

- A binding cable
- An ESC
- A servo motor (or you can use a BLDC motor too, but it is too risky; I don't recommend it while binding the transmitter to the receiver)
- A battery

Firstly, connect the binding cable to the RC receiver on the BAT pin, as follows. In some models, the BAT pins might be known as B/VCC:

Now, take an ESC and connect the signal, 5V, and ground pin to the CH1 pins.

Remember, the outer pin of a row is for the ground, the middle pin is for 5V, and the inner pin is for the signal.

Connect the battery to the ESC. The ESC will make a beeping sound and the RC receiver will show an LED blinking. Now, turn on the RC transmitter after installing the battery to it. Press and hold the **Bind Range Test** button until the LED of the RC receiver stops blinking. Do this process again if the LED does not stop blinking. You can try switching off and on the transmitter, and then finally disconnect the binding cable from the RC receiver.

If you have successfully bound the transmitter to the receiver, you can now test your transmitter by connecting a few servo motors to the RC receiver and moving the throttle, roll pitch, or yam of the transmitter. If successfully bound, the servo will rotate, as per the rotation of the knobs or gimbal of the transmitter.

Know the aerodynamics needed for flying a drone

Just imagine your drone produces infuriating noises. Do you know why? It is because of the BLDC motors and the propellers, right? But theoretically, drones should not make that much loud a noise. Can you imagine why? Because of the proper uses of the aerodynamics inside a drone. The physics for flying a drone is really necessary to be known by all the drone pilots because, if you cannot master the air, your drone will not fly properly. Refer to the following figure to get a rough idea on how air is effected by the propellers of the drone.

The figure is taken from the NASA website. They simulated the aerodynamics via computers:

So, basically a drone (specially quadcopters) has two pairs of propellers (two in a clockwise direction and another two in a anticlockwise direction). The speed of each motor is individually controlled to control the movement of the drone. We need to think about two things for flying a drone, the torque, and the thrust. So what are these?

Well, a torque is nothing but a twisting force that tends to cause rotation. Alternatively, we can say, in physics, the capability of rotating an object around a fixed axis is known as torque. It is symbolized as τ (Tau). Mathematically, torque is the vector product of force (F) and the distance (r) of the axis. So, we can write:

$$\vec{\tau} = \vec{F} \times \vec{r}$$

or

$$\tau = Fr\sin\theta$$

Where θ is the angle between the force and the distance from the center of the axis. We will know more about torque a little bit later. Let's speak about thrust now. Thrust is simply pushing something suddenly or with propulsive force. In physics, thrust is defined as the forward force that impels it to go faster or keeps it going in the intended direction. Mathematically, thrust is the product of pressure (P) and area (A).

So, we can say, *Thrust = P x A*.

We use a small control board to control the drone. The control board has a few sensors that provide the necessary signals to move the propellers at the proper speed, and in the right direction. Inside the control board, there is a gyroscope and accelerometer that provide the orientation information of the drone. The RC receiver gets a signal from the RC transmitter and sends it to the microcontroller of the control board, and the ESCs connected to the microcontroller are then controlled to provide the necessary speed. The following figure shows the forces and movements of the quadcopter:

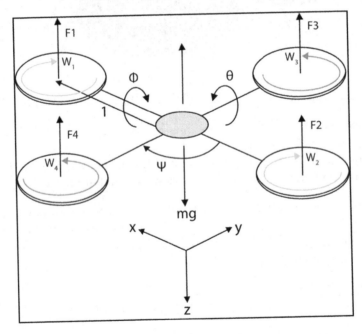

Mathematically, Thrust (T) will be proportional to the square of the angular velocity (w) of the propellers. The thrust is perpendicular to the Z direction of the drone. So, we can write:

$$T \propto \omega^2$$

or

$$T = K_a \times \omega^2$$

Here, K_a is a constant. As the propellers rotate and create a thrust in the Z direction, there must be an opposite force in the drone. Let the movement be M_i, which will also be equal to the right side of the previous equation.

Therefore, $M_i = K_b \times \omega^2$, where K_b is a constant. We used two different constants because the force might be slightly decreased or increased, due to the friction of the air particle or the dust.

The opposite pair of propellers are M_x and M_y. According to the definition of movements, if the distance of the center of the drone and a propeller is l, we can write the following equations:

$$M_x = |F_1 - F_2| \times l$$

$$M_y = |F_3 - F_4| \times l$$

The weight of the drone $W = mg$. The weight always acts in the direction of the quadcopter. From Newton's second law of motion, we know:

$$force = mass \times acceleration\ (linear)$$

The torque can be defined with the help of inertia as follows:

$$Torque = Inertia \times acceleration\ (angular)$$

Hovering

To hover the quadcopter, the weight of the drone must be equal to all the upward forces of the propellers, where the movement must be equal to zero:

$$mg = F_1 + F_2 + F_3 + F_4$$

For flying, the upward force must be greater than the weight. So, if we subtract the mass of the drone from the upward forces of the propellers, we will get the equation of motion of the drone flying. Let's say it is D_*. So, we can write:

$$D_* = F_1 + F_2 + F_3 + F_4 - mg$$

Rising or climbing or taking off

To fly the drone over the ground, the equations will be changed as follows:

$$mg < F_1 + F_2 + F_3 + F_4$$

$$D_* = F_1 + F_2 + F_3 + F_4 - mg > 0$$

Dropping or descent or falling

The drone will not fly if the weight is more than the upward forces or $D_* < 0$:

$$mg > F_1 + F_2 + F_3 + F_4$$

$$D_* = F_1 + F_2 + F_3 + F_4 - mg < 0$$

Yaw

Yaw is the motion of the drone in the xy plane, or the horizontal plane as shown in the previous figure. The opposite kind of pair of propellers will create reaction movements. If the sum of all the movements of each propeller is equal to each other, then there is no yaw motion. But if there is difference movements between any pair of propellers, there will be yaw motion, and the drone will move, as shown in the following figure:

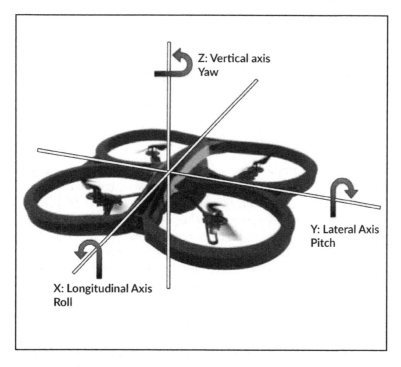

If the drone simply rotates along the z direction, it is known as a yaw motion. This will occur, if there is a stable upward force and the propeller forces are as follows:

$$I_{zz} = M_1 + M_2 + M_3 + M_4$$

Here, M_1, M_2, M_3 and M_4 are the movements of the propellers.

Pitch and roll

The pitch is the rotation of the drone in the Y direction, while the rotation along the X direction is known as roll or vice versa, depending on the front of the drone. This will happen if one pair of opposite propellers provide, thrust more than the other two propellers.

This is the simple aerodynamics of a quadcopter. We will know more details about the aerodynamics throughout this book, in the coming chapters.

Saving your drone from crashing

You hardly can prevent your drone from crashing and breaking some of the propellers, or even the body. The damage will depend on the crash and the height it falls from. It will also depend on the surface your drone lands on or crashes.

The best place to fly a drone is open fields where there are no trees or any electrical wires hanging. Do not uplift the drone with high throttle at first, increase the throttle gradually. We will know about safe throttling later. For now, you can use the Stabilize mode first. Just remember, throttle is nothing but speeding up the velocity of the propellers of the drone. If you are a beginner, my suggestion is to learn how you can levitate your drone above the ground. Once you master hovering the drone, increase the throttle a little bit. Practice more with that high. Increase the height gradually. Then, start doing the yawing to the drone. It will rotate the drone in parallel to the surface, up above the ground. Once you can yaw your drone, you can then pitch it to a forward direction or a backward direction. Then, learn how to roll the drone. From my personal experience, when I flew my first DIY drone, I became nervous about which knob/gimbal does the throttle or which one does roll/pitch and crashed my drone in the ground after 2 seconds of flying, and ended up breaking it. I can remember that the drone suddenly gave a thrust to the ground and flew about 10/12 feet up. Then I did something more horrible. I rotated the roll and pitch gimbal of the transmitter 360 degrees and the drone fell from above and landed on a rock.

So, never get nervous, do not press any button of the transmitter without knowing its task; also be careful about the weather conditions, obstacles, and air flow. That is how you can avoid most of the crashes.

Check things before flying

There are a few things you must check before flying a drone. Here is a checklist for flying a drone safely:

- Check all the connections
- Check transmitter and receiver bindings
- Check the battery charge and voltage
- Check whether all the propellers are attached tightly
- Check all the motor mountings
- Check all the screws
- Check the balance of the drone to see if any side is heavier than the other
- Always unplug the battery after flying; only attach the battery few a seconds before flying
- Check any obstacles outside
- Keep children away from the flying area
- Keep a distance from the drone while you first throttle it
- Turn on autopilot and return to the home/launch feature if they are available
- Do not fly a drone with unbalanced propellers or broken propellers
- Always wear safety glasses
- Maintain security protocols

Check the security protocols for flying a drone outside

There are some rules by the government of the country where you fly things in the sky, specially the drone. Always check the security protocols. A few common rules are as follows:

- You cannot fly a drone within 5 miles of an airport
- You must keep the drone within your eyesight
- You are not allowed to go higher than 400 feet (around 0.12 km)
- You cannot fly a drone in busy traffic areas

- You must register your drone if you use it for business purposes or professionally; you must have a license
- Always know the local rules before flying a drone

Summary

In this chapter, we have learned how we can assemble a basic drone or quadcopter. We have also learned about the aerodynamics of flying drones, some rules of not crashing drones, and the security protocols of flying drones.

In Chapter 3, *Preparing Your Drone for Flying*, we will learn how we can configure and tweak our quadcopter with proper modules and software to make it ready to fly, and then fly our first drone. I hope that will be really exciting for you. Let's start building and flying the quadcopter in Chapter 3, *Preparing Your Drone for Flying*.

3

Preparing Your Drone for Flying

As you are reading this chapter, I assume you have assembled your DIY quadcopter and now you want to program it for flying. In this chapter, we will make our drone ready for flying. But as I said before, you can use an awesome Wi-Fi module, ESP8266, as the Wi-Fi telemetry device to receive data from your drone to your computer. In this chapter, we will learn about using the ESP8266 module with our ArduPilot and Arduino, so that you can use an ESP8266 wherever you need to. We will also learn about calibrating our quadcopter and configuring our ArduPilot software. Some of the things in the following list will be discussed in this chapter too:

- Types of software to control and program the Arduino
- How we can connect the ESP8266 to the Arduino board
- Details about the ESP8266 module
- Coding for the ESP8266
- Controlling the ESP8266 from a smartphone
- Calibrating the drone after connecting the ArduPilot

So let's get started.

What is ESP8266?

Basically, an ESP8266 is a Wi-Fi module. It has the capability for 2.4 GHz Wi-Fi, which is `802.11 b/g/n`. It supports WPA and WPA2. It is a system-on chip integrated with a 32-bit processor which runs 80 MHz (it can also be overclocked to 160 MHz). It has 64 KB of RAM and a 64 KB boot ROM. The data RAM of ESP8266 is 96 KB. It is cheap, small, and powerful. That's why everyone uses it for different kinds of projects.

You can use an ESP8266 almost everywhere you need to make IoT wireless and smart. The following image is an ESP8266 with its pin out:

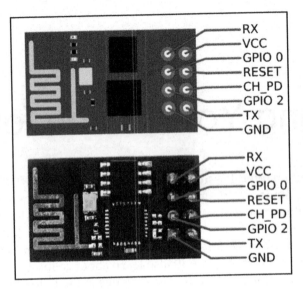

The standard ESP8266 has eight pins, as shown in the previous diagram. Let's look at their details:

- **Pin**: Function
- **RX**: It receives data
- **VCC**: Power pin (usually 3.3V maximum)
- **GPIO 0**: General purpose input output pin 0
- **RESET**: It is a reset pin
- **CH_PD**: Chip power down pin
- **GPIO 2**: General purpose input output pin 2
- **TX**: It transmits data
- **GND**: Ground pin

Connecting the ESP8266 to Arduino

Let's connect our ESP8266 to an Arduino board. You can use any Arduino. Just follow the following pin configuration. We are going to control an LED with the ESP8266. So the pin settings will be as follows:

ESP8266	Arduino
RX	3
TX	2
VCC	3V
CH_PD	3V
GPIO 0	No connection
GPIO 2	No connection

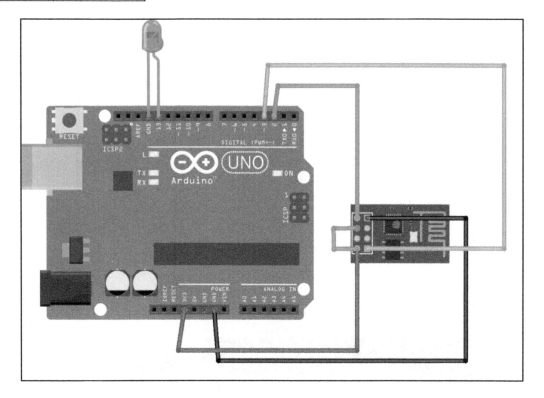

We will use an app on our smartphone to control the LED turn on and turn off functions. Add an LED on pin 13 of the Arduino for avoiding complexities for the first time. First of all, download and install the Arduino IDE from `https://www.arduino.cc/en/Main/Software`. Now you need to install a library on your Arduino IDE. Go to `https://github.com/blynkkk/blynk-library/releases/latest` and download the latest release of the `Blynk` library in ZIP format. Install the library in the Arduino IDE from **Sketch | Include Library | Add .Zip Library**:

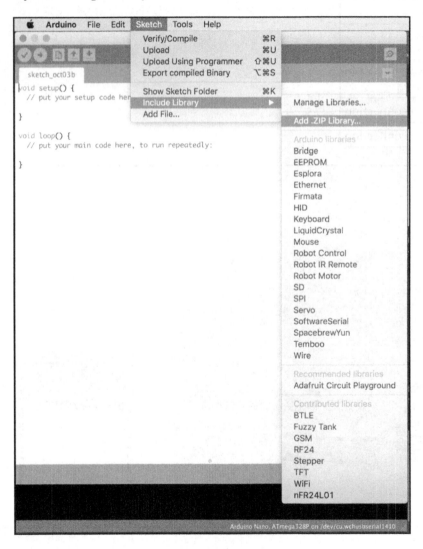

If you get an error like the following image, don't worry; just unzip the zipped file and copy all the contents of the `libraries` folder to the `Arduino IDE library` folder. The library location is as follows:

- **On Mac**: Right-click on the Arduino app icon and click on the **Show Package Contents** | **Contents** | **Java** | **libraries**
- **On Windows**: Go to **Program Files** or **Program Files (x86)** | **Arduino** | **Libraries**
- **On Linux**: Go to **User** | **Share** | **Arduino** | **Libraries**:

Specified folder/zip file does not contain a valid library | Copy error messages

Specified folder/zip file does not contain a valid library

9   Arduino Nano, ATmega328P on /dev/cu.wchusbserial1410

 You might need to update the board manager URL for the ESP8266. To do that, please follow the official guide from here: `https://github.com/esp8266/Arduino`.

Once you have installed the library and connected the ESP8266 to the Arduino, now is the time to download the Blynk mobile application. The application is available on both the App Store and Play Store. Install the application and finish the registration process, if required.

You will see the following page after the installation:

Refer to the following steps:

1. Click on **New Project** and name your project anything you want.
2. Choose the device, Arduino Uno (or your own device) and connection type, WiFi:

3. You will get a prompt that an authentication code was sent to your email, which can also be found on the project setting of the Blynk application. Ignore it for now. Swipe right ride of your screen to access the **Widget** menu and select a **Button** from there:

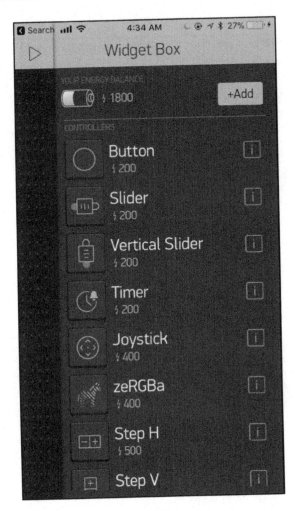

4. You will get a **Button** on the project page. Click on the **Button** and set the button properties. Select a pin type, **Digital,** and pin number 13, as we have connected our LED on the Arduino pin **D13**:

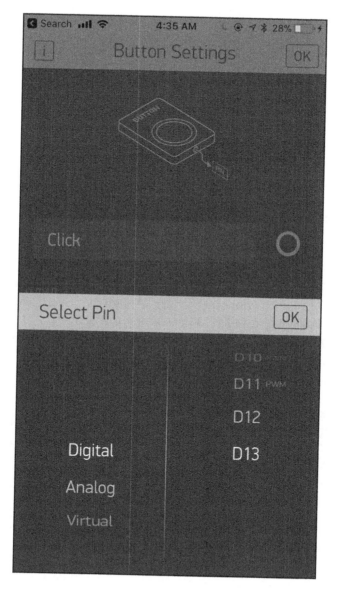

5. Now, fire up your Arduino IDE and write the following code there:

```
#define ESP8266_BAUD 9600
#include <ESP8266_Lib.h>
#include <BlynkSimpleShieldEsp8266.h>
#include <SoftwareSerial.h>
char auth[] = "YourAuthToken";
char ssid[] = "YourNetworkName";
char pass[] = "YourPassword";
SoftwareSerial EspSerial(2, 3);
ESP8266 wifi(&EspSerial);
void setup()
{
   Serial.begin(9600);
   EspSerial.begin(ESP8266_BAUD);
   delay(10);
   Blynk.begin(auth, wifi, ssid, pass);
}
void loop()
{
   Blynk.run();
}
```

6. Remember the authentication token you got in the email? Assign the value of the auth[] string with your assign token. Assign the ssid[] and pass[] strings with your Wi-Fi name and Wi-Fi password, respectively.

7. Verify and upload the code to the Arduino and open the Blynk app.

8. From the Blynk app, press the **Button** and if everything is OK, the LED connected on your Arduino should turn on.

Since you can now control an LED with your smartphone, you can now control a motor with your phone, right? For more about the Blynk code and documentation, go to www.blynk.cc. You can use tons of things with your ESP8266 using Blynk. Let's go back to our drone, which needs to be configured.

Downloading and installing APM Planner or Mission Planner

As we have been using ArduPilot as the control board of our drone, we need to use the APM Planner software for configuring our drone. Let's download APM Planner from here: `http://firmware.ardupilot.org/`, and download AMP Planner 2.0 or Mission Planner:

After successful installation, open the APM Planner or Mission Planner. The interface will look like this:

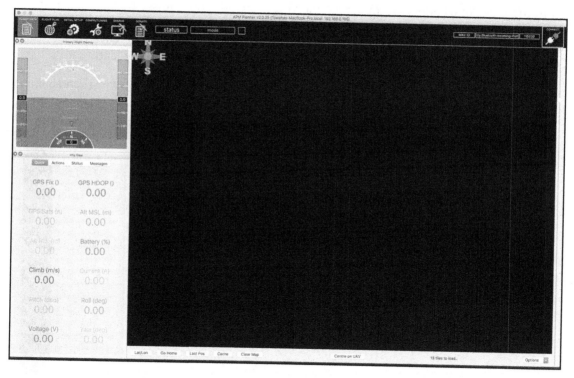

At the top left, you can see the following six menus:

- Flight data
- Flight plan
- Initial setup

- Config/tuning
- Graphs
- Donate

The option names are self-explanatory. At the top right, you can see a **Connect** button. Before the **Connect** button, you can find the **MAV ID** option, which allows you to select the right port for your ArduPilot connected to your computer by USB or by telemetry. In Windows, you can select **Auto** mode to find out the perfect port number, if you are not sure which is the COM port number. But on OSX, you need to figure out the perfect port.

For the first time, we need to connect our ArduPilot via USB to your computer. Remember to unplug the drone battery, if you are connecting via USB. You will see that the LEDs are blinking on the ArduPilot. This means your ArduPilot is getting powered. Now on your computer, open APM Planner or Mission Planner, select the **MAV ID**, and click on **Connect**. If you are not sure which is the correct **MAV ID**, then follow my lead:

1. On OSX, you will see the **Serial Port** name, as shown in the following screenshot:

2. Select `cu.usbmodem1411`. The last number may be changed for your computer. Select a baud rate of **115,200** for a higher speed and click on **Connect.**

3. Once connected, you will see some messages under the **Info View** panel of the APM Planner.

On Linux, you will see almost the same but in Windows you will see the **Port number** on the top-right side. Carefully choose the port number before clicking the **Connect** button of the software. Or you can choose **Auto** on the Mission Planner version for Windows.

Configuring the quadcopter

Let's configure our quadcopter. Before going any further with the configuration, remove all the propellers of your drone. It can be dangerous if the propellers are connected. Connect the USB cable to the ArduPilot and connect it to your computer. Open APM Planner and go to the **Initial Setup** tab. Remember, you need to disconnect the connection before going to the **Initial Setup** tab or you might see some errors (especially when installing new firmware). You will see the options, as shown the following screenshot:

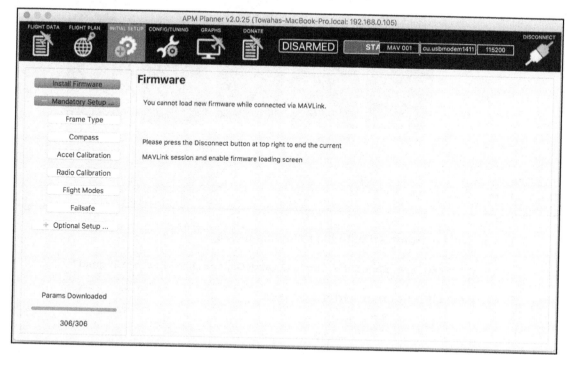

Firstly, we are going to install the firmware, which is the most important work for configuring the ArduPilot:

1. Disconnect the connection between the ArduPilot and your computer by clicking the **Disconnect** button but keep the USB cable connected.

2. Click on **Install Firmware** from the left-hand side. You will be shown several types of drones.

3. Since we are configuring a quadcopter, select the quadcopter. In my case, it is **ArduCopter 3.2.1**. The version may vary depending on the version of the ArduPilot control board:

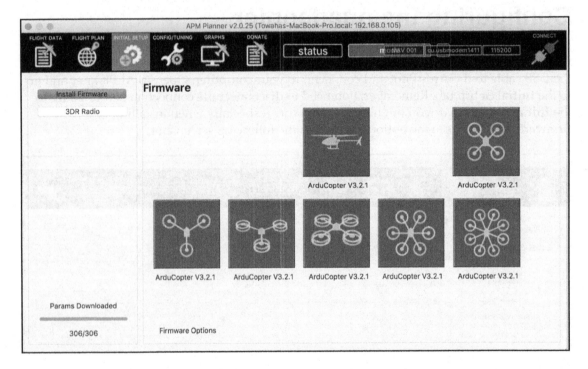

4. You will be prompted with the following message:

   `"You are about to install ArduCopter.hex for apm2-quad"`

5. Click the **OK** button to start the process.

Make sure the USB cable is connected firmly and properly.

6. After clicking **OK**, you will see that the download has begun. To see the output, you may check the **Show Output** option.

7. After downloading, the firmware will be flashed into the ArduPilot automatically. Do not unplug or loosen the connections. After successful flashing, you will see the following messages:

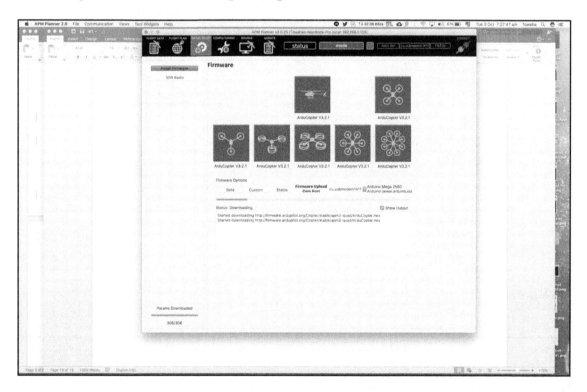

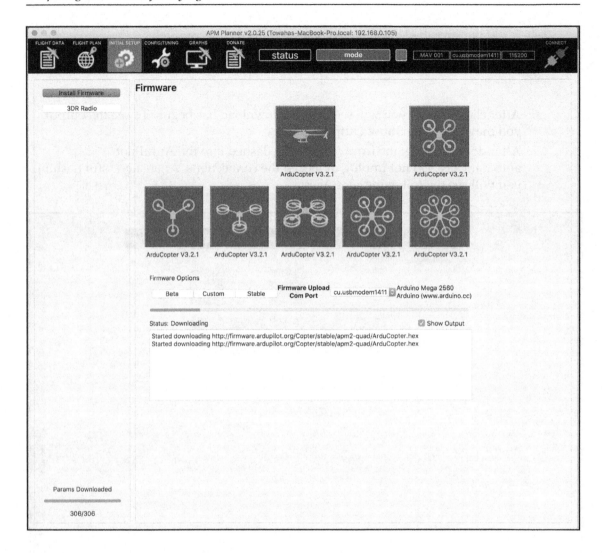

Frame type selection

Now, click the **Connect** button and go to the **Initial Setup** tab. From the **Fame Type** option, select the x shape (be aware that the four propellers are on each corner of the shape of x) quadcopter, as our ArduPilot is connected like x's center but pointed forward in between the middle of the two hands of the quadcopter:

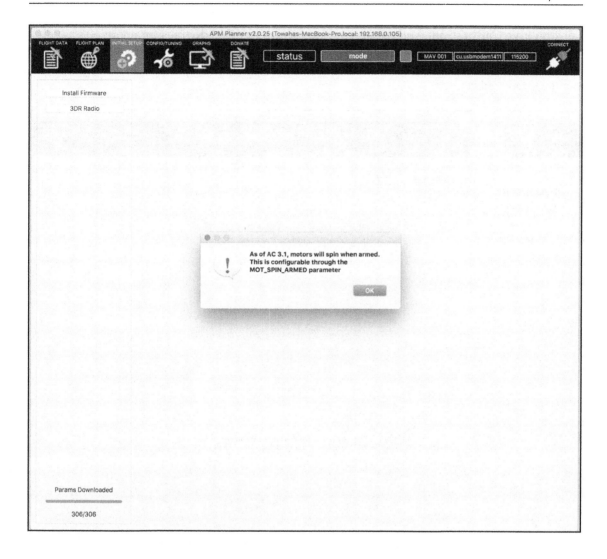

Compass calibration

Then, go to the compass and check the following options:

- Enable
- Auto detection

Click on **Live Calibration**. And rotate your quadcopter all 360 degrees for about 60 seconds. The software will collect a few calibration points for calibrating the compass to the ArduPilot. You may rotate only the ArduPilot by removing other parts from it, if you want to get a good calibration:

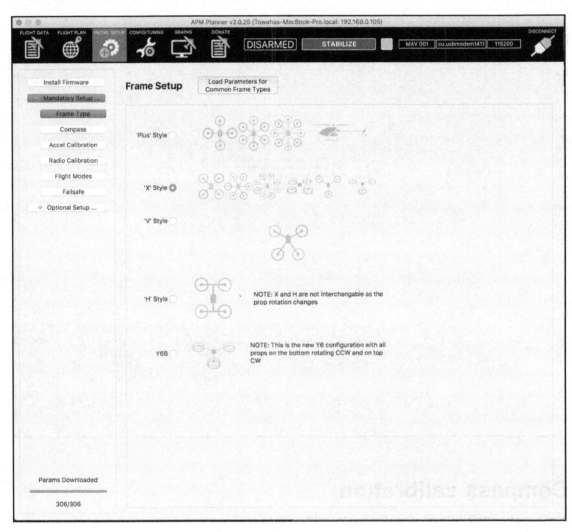

After successful calibration, you will see the following message:

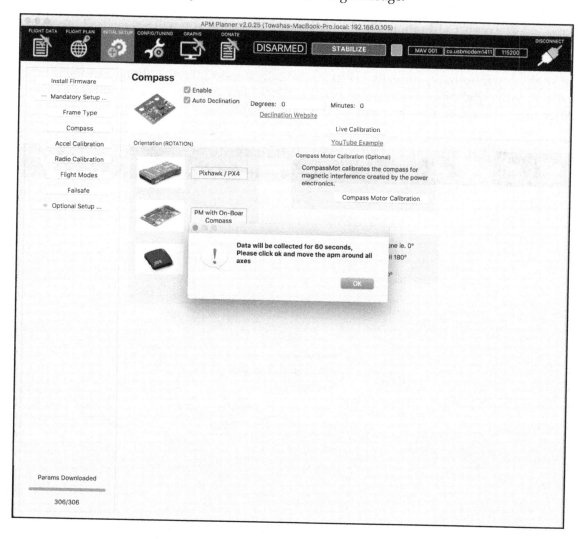

Access calibration

Now, select **Access Calibration**. Hit the **Calibrate** button and you will see instructions as to which orientation you should place your drone. Hit any key or a button. Just do what the software says and complete the calibration. Make sure you choose the orientation (above-left-right-down-up-back) correctly because it is really important when flying a drone. And make sure the USB cable is firmly connected and does not disconnect while calibrating. After successful calibration, you will see the following message:

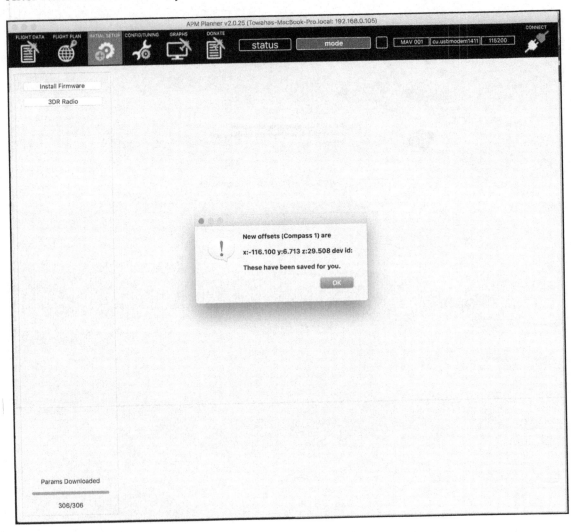

Radio calibration

As we bound our radio with our transmitter in the Chapter 2, *Assembling Your Drone*, we need to connect it to the ArduPilot and click on **Radio Calibration**. You will see the following screen:

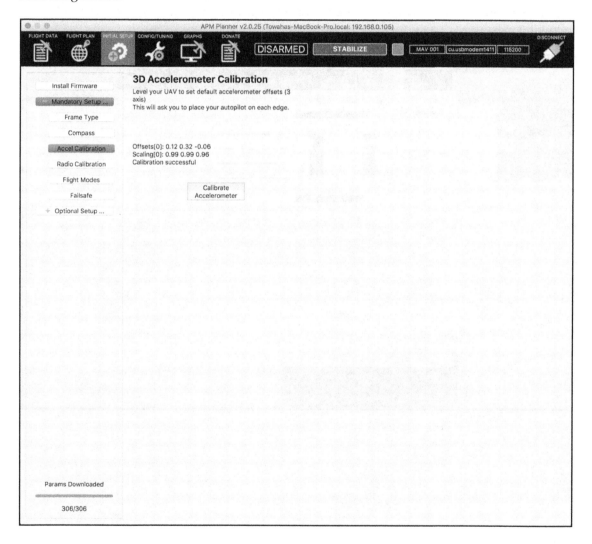

Now, choose a flying mode which is suitable to you. Make sure the transmitter is turned on. I prefer **Mode 2**. Now click on **Calibrate** and rotate all the gimbals and knobs to every position. You will see that the progress bars will show the increments and decrements while you move the gimbals and knobs. After doing this, click the **End Calibration** button. Remember, you must disconnect all the motors and propellers for this calibration or you might get a serious injury. After clicking the **End Calibration** button, you will see the following message:

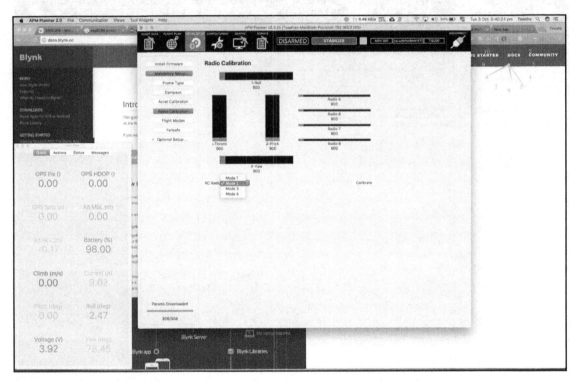

After clicking the **OK** button, you will see your calibrated settings for your transmitter and radio, as shown in the following screenshot:

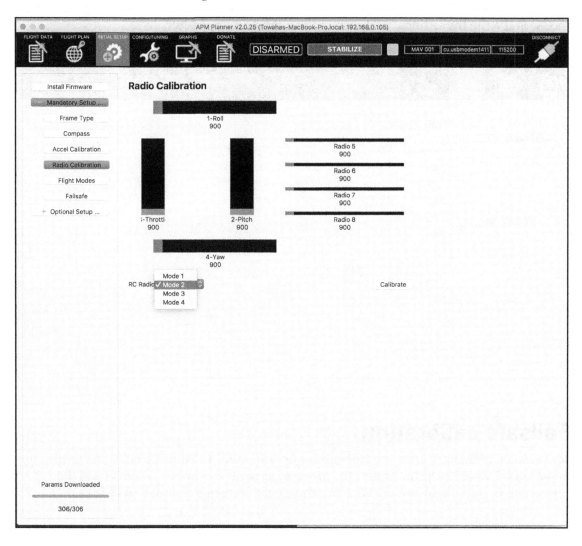

Flight mode calibration

For the flight mode, you can choose any type you want. But to avoid complexities, you can choose and write the settings, as shown in the following screenshot:

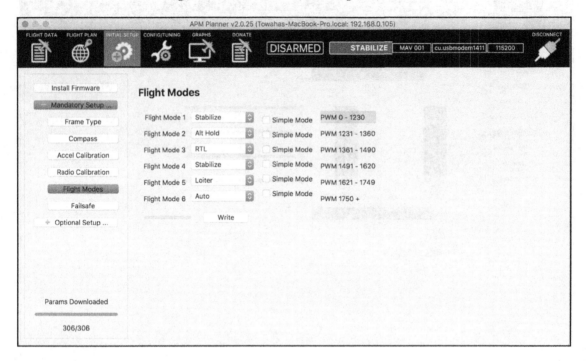

Failsafe calibration

My personal preference is for the **Failsafe** configuration for the throttle fail when returning to the land. **Failsafe** helps to protect the drone so as to avoid crashes when it loses the connection from the transmitter. You may choose the **Return to Launch** (**RTL**) option too:

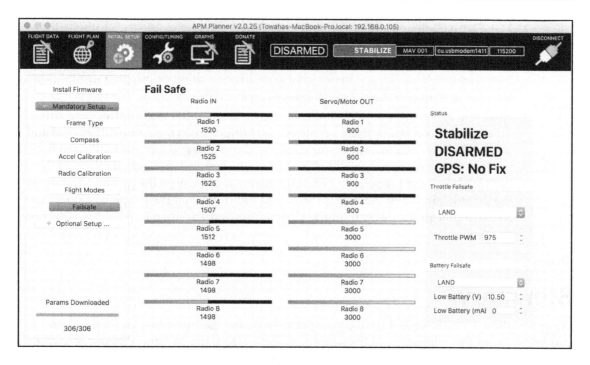

There are other optional calibrations you may need in the future. But for now, your drone is ready to fly.

Let's reconnect all the propellers and motors carefully and find a suitable place where you can test your first flight:

1. Turn on your transmitter first. Connect the battery on your drone and you will hear beeps from the ESCs. Now if everything is OK, you move the left gimbal (throttle) to the bottom right and hold it until the propellers start rotating. Keep your finger away from the other gimbal for now.

2. Make sure all the propellers are moving, now you can throttle the motors a little bit more, but don't be quick; do it gradually. Whenever the thrust is greater than the drone weight, your drone will start hovering, as we learned in the Chapter 2, *Assembling Your Drone*. Do not give your drone rolling or pitching until it is at least more than two meters away (just as an extra precaution).

3. Now you can move the pitch and roll of your transmitter and control your drone. To stop the drone from flying, remove your finger from the roll/pitch gimbal and slowly decrease the throttle. Your drone will come to ground gradually. Do not hurry, as your drone might get a bounce on the ground and get misdirected. It can also break the propellers. When the drone is almost on the ground, just push the throttle gimbal to the bottom left and hold it until all the propellers stop. As an extra precaution, switch off the transmitter first and then remove the battery of the drone.

Summary

Congratulations! You have just tried flying your drone for the first time. To fly the drone, you had to learn the calibration of the drone's modules from the Mission Planner software. You also learned how you can connect the ESP8266 and program it via the Arduino to control it via a smartphone. In Chapter 4, *Building a Follow Me Drone*, you will learn how you can build a Follow Me drone, which will follow you anywhere you go. I hope you are as excited as me to start the next chapter. See you in Chapter 4, *Building a Follow Me Drone*.

4

Building a Follow Me Drone

In Chapter 3, *Preparing Your Drone for Flying*, you learned how to build a simple DIY drone. In this chapter, we will be learning how you can give it a mind of its own. Imagine you are walking or riding a bike and a drone is following you; wouldn't that be cool?

In this chapter, we will see how we can build such a drone. In this chapter, we will also learn how we can train the drone to do something, or give the drone artificial intelligence by coding from scratch. There are several ways to build Follow Me-type drones. We will learn easy and quick ways in this chapter. Before going any further, let's learn the basics of a Follow Me drone.

What is a Follow Me drone?

A Follow Me drone follows a device or an object; the device can be your phone or a device with some sensors that continuously communicate with the drone to get the right position. If it follows an object, then there is some machine learning involved with the system. Some drones can do image processing and follow an object. For example, if you train your drone to follow dogs, you need to teach it how to detect an object and compare it with a dog and follow it, which is a little complicated. But in this chapter, you will be given some ideas that can be implemented for building your own Follow Me drone. As we were talking about following a device with the Follow Me drone, you may have guessed that the position might be determined by the GPS sensor. And, of course, you need other sensors for the drone to locate your position correctly; thus, the receiver and sender create a communication between them and follows the device. The speed of communication also needs to be faster in some cases, because you know what happens when you are walking and your pet dog is not following you. Follow Me drones are like air dogs to me. Simply, they can follow something, and they can do some simple things such as taking photos or recording videos.

If your drone is capable of doing complex things like face detecting, object targeting, and so on. then the processing speed of the drone's brain should be higher than the communication speed between the RC receiver and the drone.

Making a Follow Me drone using ArduPilot

It is super easy to build a Follow Me drone using ArduPilot. You just need to change some settings and buy a USB dongle, which is a GPS receiver. There are a few types of USB dongles that go with ArduPilot, but the official one to use is the GlobalSat ND-100S USB GPS dongle, or you can use a USB dongle or a GPS-embedded Bluetooth module such as the GlobalSat BT-368i Bluetooth GPS receiver. The following picture shows both types of modules:

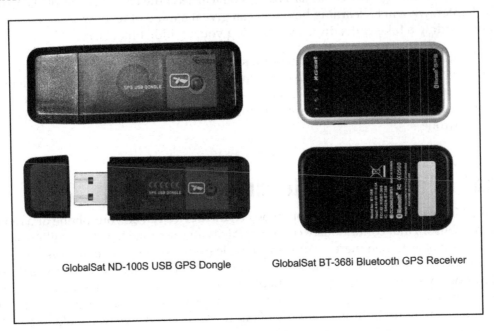

GlobalSat ND-100S USB GPS Dongle   GlobalSat BT-368i Bluetooth GPS Receiver

You will also need telemetry for setting up the modules with the ArduPilot software. Setting up the modules is easy:

1. Firstly, take your drone to a suitable place for flying and connect it via MAVLink using telemetry.
2. Now, connect your USB dongle or Bluetooth receiver to your laptop.

Make sure the dongle is connected and powered from the USB port of your laptop.

3. You can check if your module is working by using the software of the module you use, or the LED built on it.

4. Set the GPS position locked before the take off or increasing the throttle speed. Now, gradually take off the drone and keep it at a sufficient altitude (I suggest at least 7-8 feet), and switch the flying mode to Loiter. For those who do not know what the Loiter mode is, you may check the upcumming note. This will lock the drone in to position.

5. Now, on your Mission Planner software, go to the **Flight Data Screen** and right-click any position you want and select **Fly to Here**. If your drone flies to the place you just selected, then your Follow Me drone is almost ready.

6. Now, if everything works, on the Mission Planner click *Ctl+F* or *Command+F* to open a setting and click the **Follow Me** button.

7. When you click the **Follow Me** button, your computer will try to use the dongle you connected to it by showing a window, as follows:

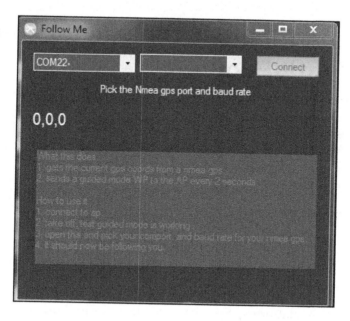

8. Select the proper COM port and the name of the device and click on **Connect**.

 Loiter mode is an automatic mode in which the copter tries to maintain the current location, the altitude, and the heading. To do this, the copter must have a good GPS receiver. In this mode, the pilot feels safe as the hand is kind of released from the sticks of the controller. You can find the settings in the Mission Planner (**Configuration** | **APM Copter** | **PIDs?** | **Loiter PID**). There, you can set up the PIDs and speed as you want. To learn more about this, you can visit http://ardupilot.org/copter/docs/loiter-mode.html.

9. Once you connect the USB dongle to the Mission Planner software, your drone will consider the dongle the **Fly to Here** location all the time.

Now, if you move with your laptop, your drone will follow your laptop. Your Follow Me drone is now ready. Why don't you walk a little bit and see if your air pet follows you? But, you might be wondering, why do I have to carry my laptop? Yes, this is irritating. You can walk with only the dongle, but the setting will be slightly different. Let's try another way of making your drone work like a Follow Me drone.

Using a smartphone to enable the Follow Me feature of ArduPilot

You can make your drone follow you if you use a smartphone. Your smartphone already has a built-in GPS, and the drone will follow your phone if properly configured. You will need an OTG connector to connect the telemetry to your phone. Wherever you take your phone, your drone will follow it, as long as the data transmission is good. You can use any of the following two applications (there might be other applications that I have not tested) for this:

- DroidPlanner2
- Tower

Unfortunately, neither of the applications is available for iPhone (there is the 3DR Solo application for iPhone that can be used to control the on-drone camera by using Wi-Fi and Sidepilot, which is able to configure the drone to Follow Me mode if you use the ArduCopter or 3DR Solo platforms). So, we need to use Android phones. Let's learn how you can configure your drone with your smartphone. Firstly, we will learn how you can configure by using the DroidPlanner 2 application.

Using DroidPlanner 2

Let's see how to use DroidPlanner 2:

1. First of all, go to the Play Store and download and install DroidPlanner 2
   (`https://play.google.com/store/apps/details?id=org.droidplanner&hl=en`).
   After installation, open the app and you will see the following page:

2. Now, connect your OTG cable/converter to your phone and connect the USB telemetry, such as SiK Telemetry Radio, to your phone via the OTG. You may see the following message:

3. Click **OK** there or your telemetry won't be powered from your phone.

4. You may need to change some settings of the application before connecting the drone. Go to the settings menu of the application (top-left corner) and select the vehicle type as **ArduCopter**:

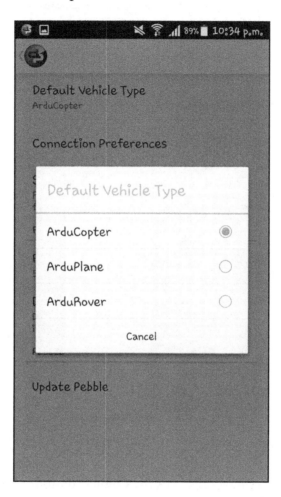

5. And from the home menu, select **Loiter** as the flight mode. You can change it while flying too:

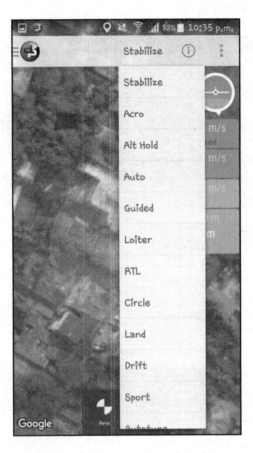

6. Now, take your drone to a suitable place for flying. Arm your drone and set the mode to **Loiter**.
7. While the drone is hovering, click the **Connect** button at the bottom of the application on your phone.
8. Once the connection is established between your drone and the phone, you will be able to see the following screen:

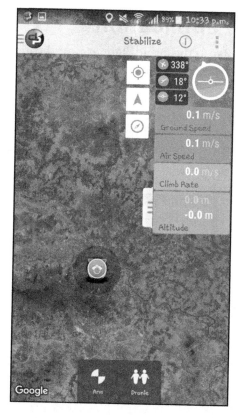

9. If you can see the preceding screen without any error, then you are ready to use your drone as a Follow Me drone. Just click the **Dronie** icon at the bottom of the screen, and your drone is now a Follow Me drone.

10. Take your phone anywhere; the drone will go with you now. You may control your drone from the application too. You can see all the flight data on the screen and know your drone's condition.

Remember, you must enable the location of your phone before using this app or this will not work.

Now we will see how we can use the Tower app for making the drone act like a Follow Me drone.

Using the Tower application

The Tower application is similar to the DroidPlanner 2 application, but has a few extra features such as camera control and smart user interface:

1. Go to the Play Store and download and install Tower (`https://play.google.com/store/apps/details?id=org.droidplanner.androi d&hl=en`). You might get a warning about the OTG connection on your screen. Just do what you need to do. After installation and connection, you will see the following page on your phone:

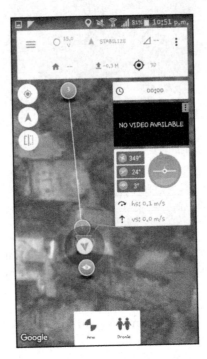

2. Now, change the flight mode to **Loiter** and click the **Dronie** button.
3. Your drone is now a Follow Me-type drone. If there is a camera connected to your drone, you will be able to see the camera signal on your phone on the **no video available** section. We will learn how to connect a camera to your drone in `Chapter 5`, *Building a Mission Control Drone*.

If you are a hardcode programmer and hardware enthusiast, you can build an Arduino drone, like the following one, and make it a Follow Me drone by enabling a few extra features. The following guidelines are not for new readers, so if you need help, you can reach me anytime. Let's get started.

Building an Arduino-based Follow Me drone

For this section, you will need the following things:

- Motors
- ESCs
- Battery
- Propellers
- Radio-controller
- Arduino Nano
- HC-05 Bluetooth module
- GPS
- MPU6050 or GY-86 gyroscope.
- Some wires

Connections are simple:

1. You need to connect the motors to the ESCs, and ESCs to the battery. You can use a four-way connector (power distribution board) for this, like in the following diagram:

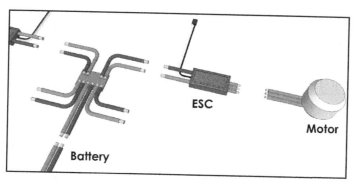

2. Now, connect the radio to the Arduino Nano with the following pin configuration:

Arduino pin	Radio pin
D3	CH1
D5	CH2
D2	CH3
D4	CH4
D12	CH5
D6	CH6

3. Now, connect the Gyroscope to the Arduino Nano with the following configuration:

Arduino pin	Gyroscope pin
5V	5V
GND	GND
A4	SDA
A5	SCL

4. You are left with the four wires of the ESC signals; let's connect them to the Arduino Nano now, as shown in the following configuration:

Arduino pin	Motor signal pin
D7	Motor 1
D8	Motor 2
D9	Motor 3
D10	Motor 4

Our connection is almost complete.

Now we need to power the Arduino Nano and the ESCs. Before doing that, making common the ground means connecting both the wired to the ground.

Before going any further, we need to upload the code to the brain of our drone, which is the Arduino Nano. The code is little bit big. I am going to explain the code after installing the necessary library. You will need a library installed to the `Arduino library` folder before going to the programming part. The library's name is `PinChangeInt`.

Install the library as you did in Chapter 3, *Preparing Your Drone for Flying*. Now, we need to write the code for the drone. The full code can be found at `https://github.com/ SOFTowaha/FollowMeDrone`.

Let's explain the code a little bit.

In the code, you will find lots of functions with calculations. For our gyroscope, we needed to define all the axes, sensor data, pin configuration, temperature synchronization data, I2C data, and so on. In the following function, we have declared two structures for the accel and gyroscope data with all the directions:

```
typedef union accel_t_gyro_union
{
  struct
    {
      uint8_t x_accel_h;
      uint8_t x_accel_l;
      uint8_t y_accel_h;
      uint8_t y_accel_l;
      uint8_t z_accel_h;
      uint8_t z_accel_l;
      uint8_t t_h;
      uint8_t t_l;
      uint8_t x_gyro_h;
      uint8_t x_gyro_l;
      uint8_t y_gyro_h;
      uint8_t y_gyro_l;
      uint8_t z_gyro_h;
      uint8_t z_gyro_l;
    } reg;
  struct
    {
      int x_accel;
      int y_accel;
      int z_accel;
      int temperature;
      int x_gyro;
      int y_gyro;
```

```
    int z_gyro;
  } value;
};
```

In the `void setup()` function of our code, we have declared the pins we have connected to the motors:

```
myservoT.attach(7); //7-TOP
myservoR.attach(8); //8-Right
myservoB.attach(9); //9 - BACK
myservoL.attach(10); //10 LEFT
```

We also called our `test_gyr_acc()` and `test_radio_reciev()` functions, for testing the gyroscope and receiving data from the remote respectively. In our `test_gyr_acc()` function. In our `test_gyr_acc()` function, we have checked if it can detect our gyroscope sensor or not and set a condition if there is an error to get gyroscope data then to set our pin 13 high to get a signal:

```
void test_gyr_acc()
{
  error = MPU6050_read (MPU6050_WHO_AM_I, &c, 1);
  if (error != 0)
    {
      while (true)
        {
          digitalWrite(13, HIGH);
          delay(300);
          digitalWrite(13, LOW);
          delay(300);
        }
    }
}
```

We need to calibrate our gyroscope after testing if it connected. To do that, we need the help of mathematics. We will multiply both the `rad_tilt_TB` and `rad_tilt_LR` by 2.4 and add it to our `x_a` and `y_a` respectively. then we need to do some more calculations to get correct `x_adder` and the `y_adder`:

```
void stabilize()
  {
    P_x = (x_a + rad_tilt_LR) * 2.4;
    P_y = (y_a + rad_tilt_TB) * 2.4;
    I_x = I_x + (x_a + rad_tilt_LR) * dt_ * 3.7;
    I_y = I_y + (y_a + rad_tilt_TB) * dt_ * 3.7;
    D_x = x_vel * 0.7;
    D_y = y_vel * 0.7;
```

```
P_z = (z_ang + wanted_z_ang) * 2.0;
I_z = I_z + (z_ang + wanted_z_ang) * dt_ * 0.8;
D_z = z_vel * 0.3;
if (P_z > 160)
   {
     P_z = 160;
   }
if (P_z < -160)
   {
     P_z = -160;
   }
if (I_x > 30)
   {
     I_x = 30;
   }
if (I_x < -30)
   {
     I_x = -30;
   }
if (I_y > 30)
   {
     I_y = 30;
   }
if (I_y < -30)
   {
     I_y = -30;
   }
if (I_z > 30)
   {
     I_z = 30;
   }
if (I_z < -30)
   {
     I_z = -30;
   }
x_adder = P_x + I_x + D_x;
y_adder = P_y + I_y + D_y;
}
```

We then checked that our ESCs are connected properly with the `escRead()` function. We also called `elevatorRead()` and `aileronRead()` to configure our drone's elevator and the aileron.

We called `test_radio_reciev()` to test if the radio we have connected is working, then we called `check_radio_signal()` to check if the signal is working. We called all the stated functions from the `void loop()` function of our Arduino code. In the `void loop()` function, we also needed to configure the power distribution of the system. We added a condition, like the following:

```
if(main_power > 750)
  {
    stabilize();
  } else
  {
    zero_on_zero_throttle();
  }
```

We also set a boundary; if `main_power` is greater than 750 (which is a stabling value for our case), then we stabilize the system or we call `zero_on_zero_throttle()`, which initializes all the values of all the directions.

After uploading this, you can control your drone by sending signals from your remote control. Now, to make it a Follow Me drone, you need to connect a Bluetooth module or a GPS. You can connect your smartphone to the drone by using a Bluetooth module (HC-05 preferred) or another Bluetooth module as master-slave usage. And, of course, to make the drone follow you, you need the GPS. So, let's connect them to our drone.

To connect the Bluetooth module, follow the following configuration:

Arduino pin	Bluetooth module pin
TX	RX
RX	TX
5V	5V
GND	GND

See the following diagram for clarification:

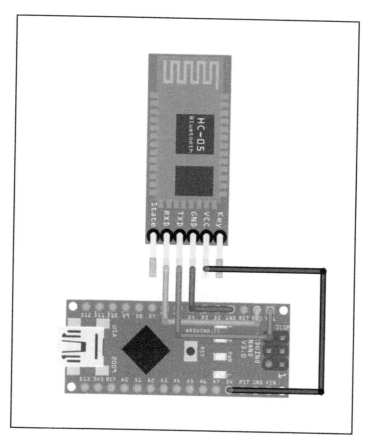

For the GPS, connect it as shown in the following configuration:

Arduino pin	GPS pin
D11	TX
D12	RX
GND	GND
5V	5V

See the following diagram for clarification:

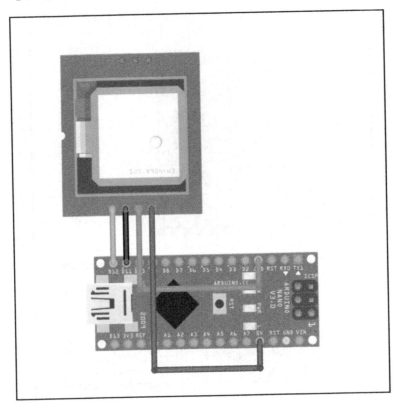

Since all the sensors usages 5V power, I would recommend using an external 5V power supply for better communication, especially for the GPS.

If we use the Bluetooth module, we need to make the drone's module the slave module and the other module the master module. To do that, you can set a pin mode for the master and then set the baud rate to at least 38,400, which is the minimum operating baud rate for the Bluetooth module. Then, we need to check if one module can hear the other module. For that, we can write our void loop() function as follows:

```
if(Serial.available() > 0)
  {
    state = Serial.read();
  }
if (state == '0')
```

```
    {
        digitalWrite(Pin, LOW);
        state = 0;
    }
else if (state == '1')
    {
        digitalWrite(Pin, HIGH);
        state = 0;
    }
```

And do the opposite for the other module, connecting it to another Arduino. Remember, you only need to send and receive signals, so refrain from using other utilities of the Bluetooth module, for power consumption and swiftness.

If we use the GPS, we need to calibrate the compass and make it able to communicate with another GPS module.

We need to read the long value from the I2C, as follows:

```
float readLongFromI2C()
    {
        unsigned long tmp = 0;
        for (int i = 0; i < 4; i++)
          {
            unsigned long tmp2 = Wire.read();
            tmp |= tmp2 << (i*8);
          }
        return tmp;
    }
float readFloatFromI2C()
    {
        float f = 0;
        byte* p = (byte*)&f;
        for (int i = 0; i < 4; i++)
        p[i] = Wire.read();
        return f;
    }
```

Then, we have to get the geo distance, as follows, where DEGTORAD is a variable that changes degree to radian:

```
float geoDistance(struct geoloc &a, struct geoloc &b)
    {
        const float R = 6371000; // Earth radius
        float p1 = a.lat * DEGTORAD;
        float p2 = b.lat * DEGTORAD;
        float dp = (b.lat-a.lat) * DEGTORAD;
```

```
        float dl = (b.lon-a.lon) * DEGTORAD;
        float x = sin(dp/2) * sin(dp/2) + cos(p1) * cos(p2)
        * sin(dl/2) * sin(dl/2);
        float y = 2 * atan2(sqrt(x), sqrt(1-x));
        return R * y;
    }
```

We also need to write a function for the Geo bearing, where `lat` and `lon` are latitude and longitude respectively, gained from the raw data of the GPS sensor:

```
float geoBearing(struct geoloc &a, struct geoloc &b)
{
  float y = sin(b.lon-a.lon) * cos(b.lat);
  float x = cos(a.lat)*sin(b.lat) - sin(a.lat)*cos(b.lat)*cos(b.lon-a.lon);
  return atan2(y, x) * RADTODEG;
}
```

You can also use a mobile app to communicate with the GPS and make the drone move with you. Then the process is simple. Connect the GPS to your drone and get the TX and RX data from the Arduino and spread it through the radio and receive it through the telemetry, and then use the GPS from the phone with DroidPlanner or Tower. You also need to add a few lines in the main code to calibrate the compass. You can see the previous calibration code. The calibration of the compass varies from location to location. So, I would suggest you use the try-error method. In the following section, I will discuss how you can use an ESP8266 to make a GPS tracker that can be used with your drone.

GPS Tracker using ESP8266

We will use the following components:

- NodeMCU (it has a built-in ESP8266)
- GPS receiver (you can use the Ublox NEO-6M GPS Module)
- A few cables
- Power source
- A smartphone (for the Blynk)

To make the connection, follow the pin configurations with NodeMCU and the GPS receiver:

NodeMCU	GPS receiver
D1	TX
D2	RX
GND	GND
VCC	3V

See the following circuit for clarification:

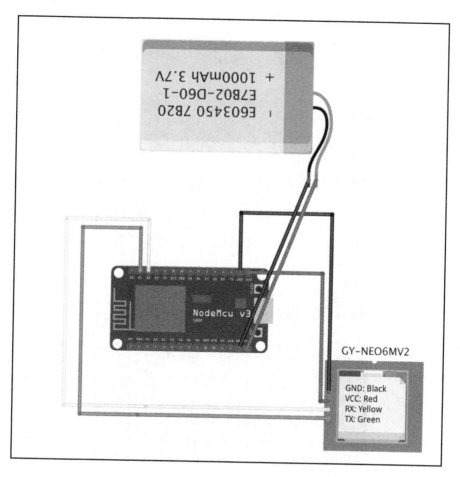

1. Now, connect the NodeMCU to the computer and open the Arduino application to program the NodeMCU. Before uploading the code, let's open our Blynk app.
2. Create a new project, as we discussed in `Chapter 3`, *Preparing Your Drone for Flying*.
3. Remember the authentication code sent to the email address you registered with the app; this will be needed later. In my case, I have set my project name as **MY GPS TRACKER**, device type as `NodeMCU`, and connection type `WiFi`, as follows:

4. To see the real-time location in text value, add two text fields with **Labeled Value**.

5. For latitude, set the pin type **Virtual** and pin **V1**:

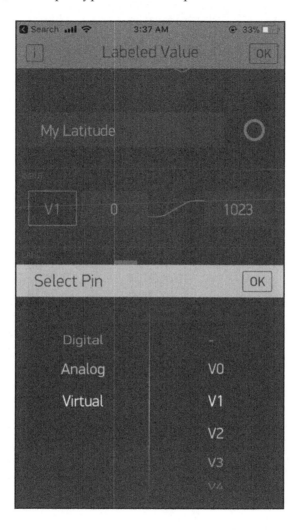

6. For longitude, select pin type **Virtual** and pin **V2**, as follows. You may change the color of the text by tapping the circular color icon:

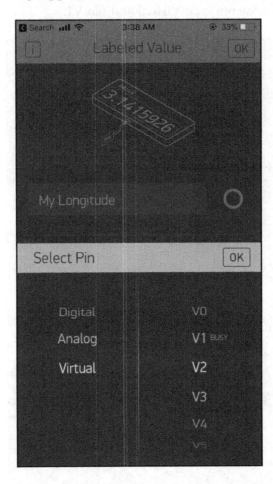

7. Now, add the map from the widget menu and select pin type to be **Virtual** and number to be **V0**:

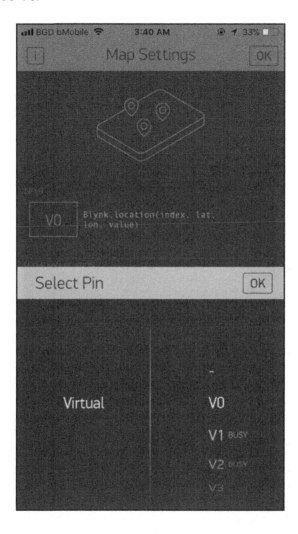

8. The Blynk application will need your permission to use your phone's GPS. You may see the following if the location service is turned off:

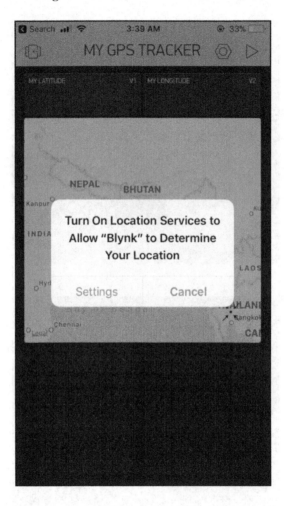

9. We may need to see how many satellites there are, so select a **Display Value** or **Labeled Value** to the screen with **Virtual** pin and **V3** configuration. Our visual should look like the following:

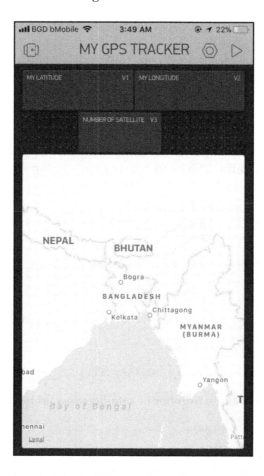

10. Now we need to code for the NodeMCU. We need to include the following libraries in our code:

```
#include <TinyGPS++.h>
#include <SoftwareSerial.h>
#include <ESP8266WiFi.h>
#include <BlynkSimpleEsp8266.h>
```

11. To add these libraries, you need to download the libraries and install them to your Arduino software. To install the libraries, go to **Sketch** | **Include Library** | **Add .zip Library** and select the folder you can download from `https://github.com/blynkkk/blynk-library/releases/download/v0.5.0/Blynk_Release_v0.5.0.zip` and `https://github.com/SOFTowaha/FollowMeDrone/blob/master/TinyGPS-master.zip`.

12. After installing the libraries, let's declare some variables, as follows:

```
#define BLYNK_PRINT Serial //for defining the Blynk Serial
static const int RX = 4, TX = 5;
static const uint32_t GPSBaud = 9600;
```

13. Form the pinout of the NodeMCU, you can see that pin 4 is actually D2 and pin 5 is D1. We declared the GPS baud rate to be 9600. If this speed does not work with your GPS, then choose a lower baud rate such as half of 9600.

14. Now, create an object for the TinyGPS:

```
TinyGPSPlus mygps;
```

15. Since we have added a virtual pin V0 for our map, we need to define it:

```
WidgetMap myMap(V0);
```

16. To start communicating, we need to pass the TX and RX value to the SoftwareSerial:

```
SoftwareSerial test_GPS(RX, TX);
```

17. The Blynk timer and the number of satellites should be declared too:

```
BlynkTimer timer;
float noofsats;
```

18. For the authentication and the Wi-Fi connection part, add the following lines:

```
char auth[] = "********"; //This key can be found on your email
char ssid[] = "********"; //Your WiFi name
char pass[] = "********"; //Your WiFi Password
```

19. Now, we will write our `void setup()` function. Inside the function, we will start our Blynk connection and check the GPS. In the `void loop()` function, we will display the latitude, longitude, and number of satellites in the Blynk. The full code can be found at `https://github.com/SOFTowaha/FollowMeDrone/blob/master/GPS_Blynk.ino`.

20. Now, upload the code to the NodeMCU after connecting it to the computer.

You can see some information on the Serial Monitor of the Arduino software. To see the real-time data only, start the project from the Blynk application and you will see your location in the Blynk:

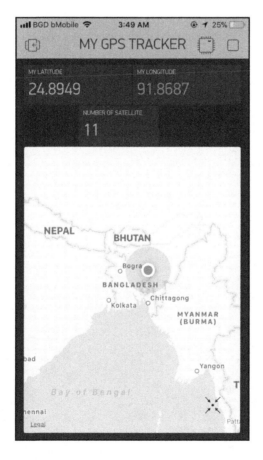

You can add the same technique to your Follow Me drone and control it from your Blynk application.

Summary

In this chapter, we have learned how we can build a Follow Me-type drone. We have learned how we can use DroidPlanner 2 and Tower to configure our drone to be a Follow Me drone. We have also learned how we can build a custom drone from scratch. In Chapter 5, *Building a Mission Control Drone,* we will do something even more exciting. We will build a mission control drone that will do a task given by you, and then return to you. I hope you will love to build one for you. So, why wait? Brace yourself for the next adventure.

5

Building a Mission Control Drone

In Chapter 4, *Building a Follow Me Drone*, we learned how we can build a Follow Me-type drone by using a smartphone or an external USB dongle. In this chapter, we will build or modify an existing drone to do something on its own. Actually, not on its own, but by our commands. Before going any further, let's discuss mission control drones.

Mission control drones are one of the common and most useful drones these days. We have seen how Amazon ships its products by such drones. They ship the packages and return to the base. The other types of mission control drones do surveys. They fly in an area and collect data. In this chapter, we will build such a kind of drone. We can do this with ArduPilot. So, let's get started.

Surveying with a drone

In Chapter 3, *Preparing Your Drone for Flying*, we have built a DIY drone using ArduPilot. We will first set up our existing drone for doing surveys. We do not need to change any kind of hardware in that system:

1. Open the Mission Planner software and go to the **Config/Tuning** page of Mission Planner and select **Planner**. You will see the following page:

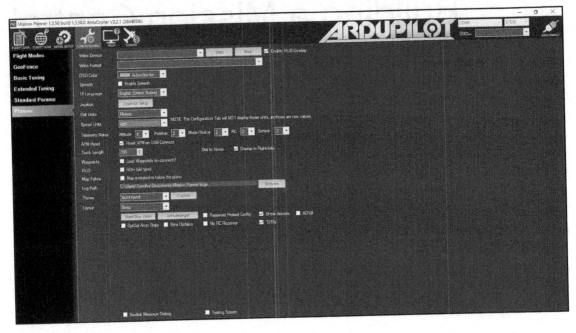

2. Now, choose a suitable unit for the distance and the speed of the copter, because these are vitally important to send a drone somewhere precisely.

3. From the top-left corner of the Mission Planner, select **Flight Plan**, and you will
   see the following screen:

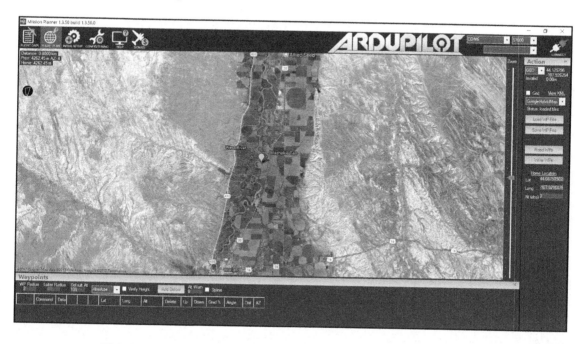

This is just a map, and you can see a green pointer which says **Home/H** when
the mouse is hovered over it. We can click and move the pointer anywhere
we want.

4. We first place the pointer from where we will depart the drone to our destination:

Remember, this is very important for a mission control drone because this is used for the returning point of the drone. So, zoom in for placing the pointer to a certain place. I chose the rooftop of my house from where I will send the drone.

5. Now, under the map screen, you can see a panel called **Waypoints**. We need to change some settings there too:

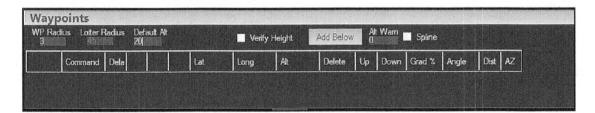

6. Set the **WP Radius** between 2 and 5 meters, and the suitable **Loiter Radius** if you use as a Follow Me drone. Select a perfect altitude in the **Default Alt** box.

   Make sure that, where the drone will fly, there are no obstacles at that height, and set the altitude slightly higher than that height. If the region is hilly, or there are some houses, then select the **Verify Height Box** for avoiding obstacles.

7. Now, we need to select a place to which we want to send our drone. I have selected three waypoints by clicking the left button of the mouse, as you can see on the following screenshot:

I want to hover my drone to these three selected points and see what is happening there and come to the place from where I launched the drone. So, I need to set the **Return to Launch** (**RTL**) option on the waypoints.

8. Click **Add Below** on the Waypoints panel and you will see a new waypoint.

Before clicking the **Add Below** button, make sure you select the last waypoint so that the next waypoint of the last destination is the RTL waypoint.

9. Then click the command menu and select the **RETURN_TO_LAUNCH** option:

10. That's it. Your survey mission control drone is ready to do the survey in the air. You need to save the waypoint file to write it to ArduPilot. To do that, right-click on the map and go to **File Load | Save | Save WP File**:

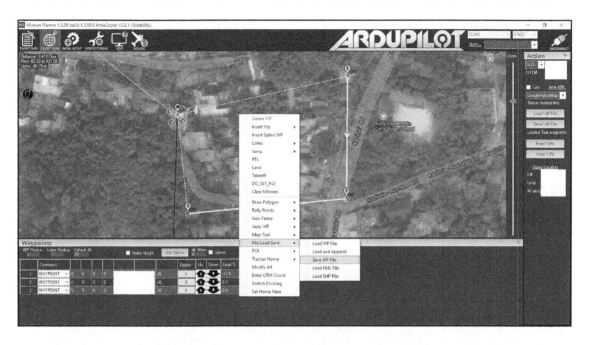

11. Give a name to your waypoint file and click on **Save**. You can reuse it by clicking the **Load WP File** on the right-side of the screen. You can change the type of the map and add some extra features to the map from the right-side of the map:

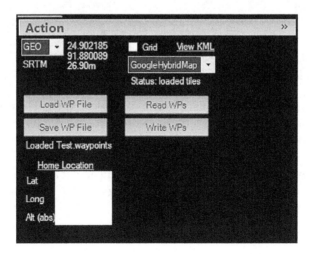

12. Now all we need to do is load the mission to ArduPilot. You can do this by connecting the drone to the computer via telemetry or USB cable. Check for the correct COM port or select the Auto mode. Now, click on the **Connect** button and select the **Load WP File** from the right-side of the map (or right-click on the map). Select the file we just saved and hit the **Write WPs** button. You will see a pop-up message, and after that your copter will memorize the places you just uploaded to it. You can erase the memory by uploading another waypoint file or resetting the waypoint:

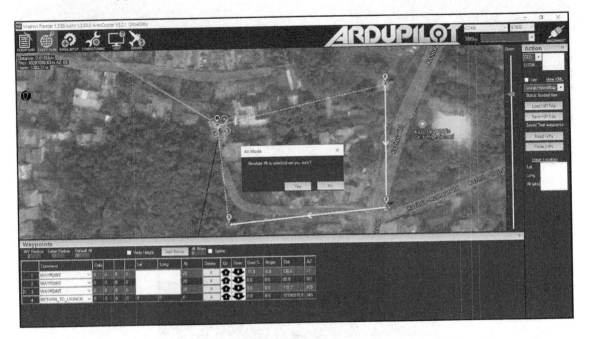

13. Now, take the drone to the place where we selected the **Home/H** point, and arm it (in auto mode). Our drone will fly to the three points we have selected and then finally it will return to the **Home/H** point. The timing of hovering depends on the speed you selected, on the **Config/Tuning** page. To select the auto mode, go to **Config/Tuning** and select **Flight Mode**. You can set any mode you want to be auto. Play with other settings too. Don't forget to hit the **Save Modes** button after changing any mode:

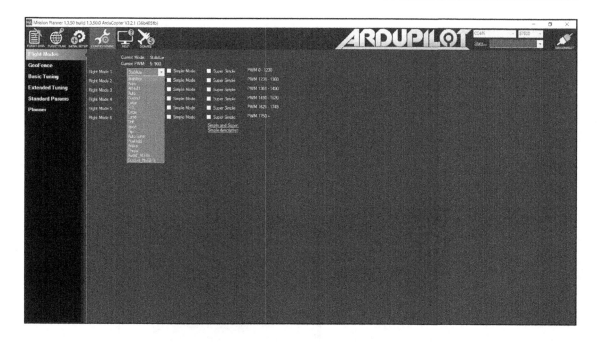

Using drones and delivery man

In this section we will ship or drop a package to a destination by our drone. This is a tricky part in the Mission Planner software. There is no direct way to do it. We can modify the camera shutter button to drop a package from our drone. We need to connect a servo motor with ArduPilot, and we will trigger a signal to the channel we connect and move the servo. If we have a placeholder connected to our servo, we can drop the package from the placeholder by triggering the servo from our remote or the Mission Planner software.

Let's connect the servo motor first. For our quadcopter, we have used one-four output channels of ArduPilot. On any other channel, we will connect a servo, as shown in the following picture:

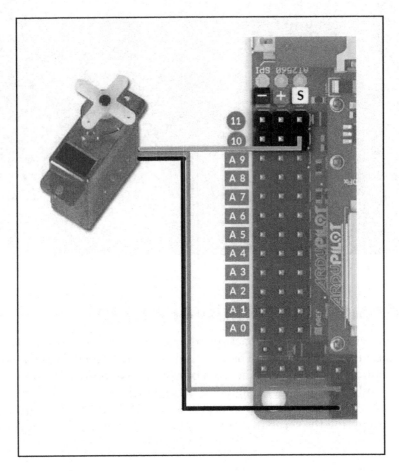

1. Now, go to the initial setup of the Mission Planner software, and from **Optional Hardware**, select **Camera Gimbal**. At the bottom you will see the camera **Shutter** option. Select an unused channel (I chose CH7) and set the **Shutter Pushed** to 1100 for a better push of the servo motor. You can also change the minimum and maximum of the servo rotation according to your need:

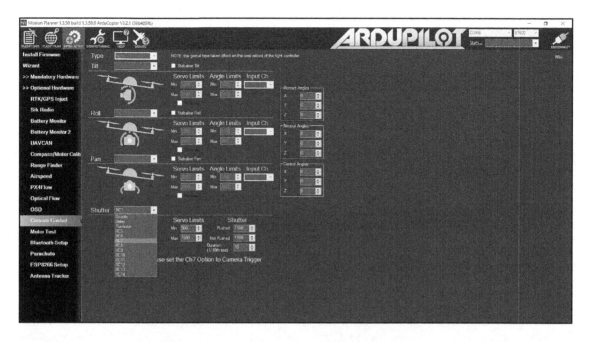

Here is a suggestion of what type of gimbal you can use to your drone:

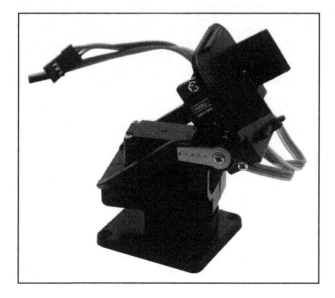

2. Now, let's get started with dropping the package to a destination. To do that, you need to select a waypoint from the **Flight Plan** menu. Then click the **Add Below** button and set it to RETURN_TO_LAUNCH. Save the waypoint file and connect your drone to the computer. Load the saved waypoint file and write it to ArduPilot. Then attach your package to your gimbal in such a way that when the gimbal is triggered by the servo, the package falls:

3. Now, arm your drone and wait for it to reach the destination. Then, from the Flight Data screen, right-click on the **map** and click the **Trigger Camera NOW** option:

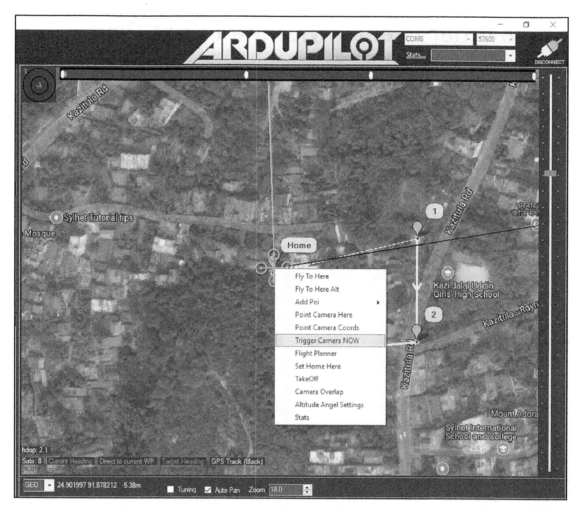

The package will be dropped at the destination and your drone will return to the launch point, as described in the waypoint.

Some other tweaks with the Flight Plan screen

You can select the waypoints from the **WayPoint** panel, as shown before. When you select a waypoint, the latitude and longitude are added to the waypoint. It means the drone will follow the position and go there by following the shortest path algorithm. We can do some actions on the location points by changing the command from the **WayPoint** panel. Please try them yourself and let me know what happens and which command you liked most.

Communicating with the drone via the ESP8266

In this chapter, we have successfully delivered a package to a place by using our mission control drone. But mission control needs to be aware of the weather and the environment for a successful flight and mission. So, if we can monitor the weather surrounding the drone, we can fly it safely and the package can be delivered without any problem.

To monitor the weather, we need the following things (for demonstration purposes, we will only look at the air pressure in this chapter):

- A barometric pressure sensor (BMP 180 preferred)
- An Arduino (pro mini preferred)
- An ESP8266 transreceiver module

Firstly, connect the Arduino to the barometer sensor. The pin configuration is as follows:

Arduino	Barometer sensor
GND	GND
VCC	VCC
A4	SCL
A5	SDA

See the following circuit diagram for further clarification:

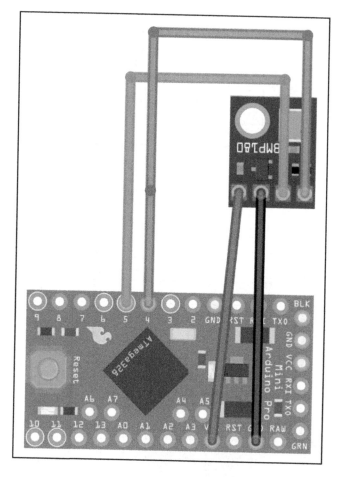

Now, connect the ESP8266 to the Arduino. The pin configuration is as follows:

Arduino	ESP8266
VCC	VCC
GND	GND
10	UTXD
11	TRXD
3	RST

See the following circuit diagram:

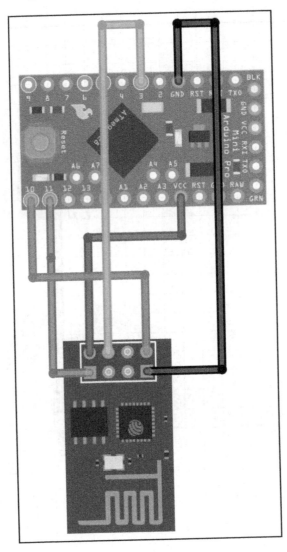

Also, we need to connect a 3.3V power supply (for example, a battery) to the system. The configuration will be as follows:

ESP8266	Power supply
VCC	3.3V
GND	GND
CH_PHD	3.3V

See the following diagram for more clarification:

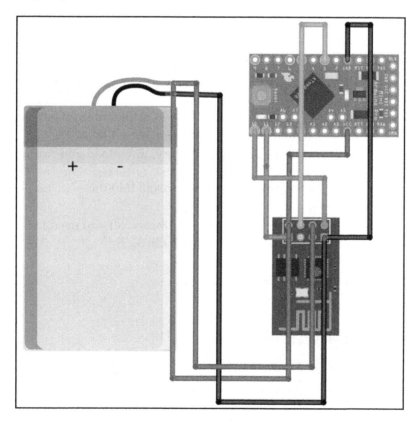

Now, we need to configure a server from which we will monitor the weather. We can use any kind of server, but I liked the EasyIoT (`https://easyiot-cloud.com/`) server:

1. Create an account there and let's get started:

   - We will upload code to our Arduino. The full source code can be found at `https://github.com/SOFTowaha/MissionControl-Drone/blob/master/BarometerCode.ino`
   - We can discuss the main functions of the code
   - We used the following libraries in our code:

     ```
     #include <Esp8266EasyIoT.h>
     #include <SFE_BMP180.h>
     #include <ESP8266WiFi.h>
     ```

   - To install the first library to Arduino, download all the files from `https://github.com/iot-playground/Arduino/tree/master/Esp8266EasyIoT` and install them from Arduino software or add them to the Arduino software's library
   - To install the barometer library, download and extract the ZIP file (`https://github.com/SOFTowaha/MissionControl-Drone/blob/master/SFE_BMP180.zip`) and install it in the `Arduino/libraries` folder
   - To install the `ESP8266WiFi` library, all you need to do that is to go to the Board Manager install ESP8266

2. From the code, define the drone's altitude:

   ```
   #define ALTITUDE
   ```

   Which is important to get correct pressure data.

3. We declared our hardware as follows:

   ```
   SFE_BMP180 bmp180;
   Esp8266EasyIoT esp;
   ```

4. The kind of data we want to see from the server needs to be defined in the code too. We want to see temperature, pressure, and forecast in the server. So, define them as follows:

```
Esp8266EasyIoTMsg msgTemp(CHILD_ID_TEMP, V_TEMP);
Esp8266EasyIoTMsg msgPress(CHILD_ID_BARO, V_PRESSURE);
Esp8266EasyIoTMsg msgForec(CHILD_ID_BARO, V_FORECAST);
```

5. Our `void setup()` function is simple. We need to set the baud rates for the ESP8266. For debugging on the Serial Monitor, we can also add another baud rate:

```
Serial1.begin(9600);
Serial.begin(115200);
```

6. We need to initialize our sensor, which is a pressure sensor. So, in the `void setup()` function, we need to check the barometer by adding a condition:

```
if (bmp180.begin())
    Serial.println("BMP180 initialization
    successful");
  else
    {
      Serial.println("BMP180 initialization
      failed\n\n");
      while(1);
    }
```

7. Here, `while(1)` will pause the system forever. Then we need to prepare the ESP8266 for other purposes by writing the following code, passing the parameters:

```
esp.begin(NULL, ESP_RESET_PIN, &Serial1, &Serial);
```

8. If the ESP8266 is connected successfully, we can pass a few other parameters to `esp.present()` to send our data to the ESP8266, and hence send it back to the server:

```
esp.present(CHILD_ID_TEMP, S_TEMP);
esp.present(CHILD_ID_BARO, S_BARO);
```

9. For the forecast, we have created a function in the code file:

```
calculateForecast(double pressure){
  }
```

Here we have set some variables and conditions, depending on the time, and get the average data and show it for the next few minutes.

The `void loop()` function is loaded with some checking with the time and status of the sensors.

10. To connect to the EasyIoT server, we need to add the following credentials at the top of the code:

```
#define AP_USERNAME "******"
#define AP_PASSWORD "******"
#define INSTANCE_ID "******"
```

11. Make sure you connect your ESP8266 to the internet. To do that, define your router's ID and password in the code and connect it. For the drone, I would recommend using a portable router:

```
const char* ssid = "The WiFi Name";
const char* password = "WiFI Password";
in the void setup() file add the following line.
WiFi.begin(ssid, password);
```

12. Now, from the EasyIot dashboard, go to **Configuration | Modules | Add Module**. Give your module an ID (you cannot edit this), a **Name,** and select **Module Type** to be generic:

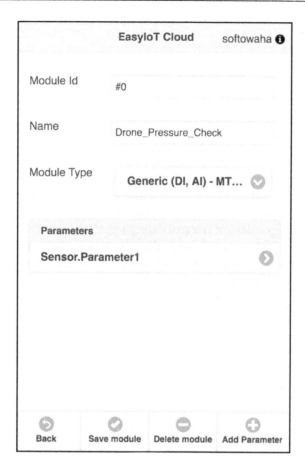

13. Save the module after adding the sensor parameters from our temperature and pressure.
14. Then go to **Config | User Info** and set the **Instance Id** for the module we have just made.
15. Now, you can upload the code to the Arduino and check the data shown in the server from the **Module** list.

Summary

In this chapter, we have learned how we can build a mission control drone and how we can communicate to the drone from the server. We also discussed adding a camera to the drone so that we can have a real view from the drone.

So, now you can drop an egg on your friend's head from the sky, right? Just kidding. To be honest, I did that when I made my first package shipping or mission control drone. You may try this. But don't try to drop something too heavy, as you know the acceleration due to gravity is heartless, and the weight of the body will be increased as much as the drone is above and the body weigh. Whatever, you can now watch from your home what other people are doing by surveying, or your can add up some sensors and collect information of a place. These are the things mission control drone usually does. There are other usages of such kinds of drones. I believe you will learn them soon. Or you can invent something new. To enhance the process of building drones in a more efficient way, we will make another exciting drone that will take a selfie of you and record a video. Will that not be wonderful? I bet you will love it. In Chapter 6, *Building a Drone to Take Selfies and Record Videos*, we will see how we can build a selfie drone that can take photos from the sky and capture videos as per your commands.

6
Building a Drone to Take Selfies and Record Videos

Have you ever thought of something that can take a photo from the air, or perhaps take a selfie from it? How about we build a drone for taking selfies and recording videos from the air? In this chapter, we will build a drone for aerial photography and videography. Don't worry; you can use it for taking selfies too. Before going on to build our photography drone, we will discuss the usages and present photography drones in the market, as well as the reason why you should build your own photography drone. We will also discuss the following topics in this chapter:

- Drone photography or aerial photography
- Connecting cameras to the drone
- Controlling cameras from the ground

So, let's get started.

Photography drones

Taking photos from the sky is one of the most exciting things in photography in the present year. You can shoot from the sky from helicopters, planes, or even from satellites. However, you know that they are not cheap or easy to utilize for taking photos, unless you have a personal air vehicle. If you have ever googled drone photography, I am sure you will definitely want to build or buy a drone for photography, because of the amazing views of the common subjects taken from the sky. If you want to see some drone photography, you can go to the following link: `https://www.flickr.com/groups/2199141@N21/pool/`.

Taking photos from a drone or making videos is really simple. All you have to do is keep the camera settings in auto mode and fly the drone wherever needed. You can control the drone from the drone controlling software or from the camera application. Just control your camera from your mobile application, take a shot and voila! Your first drone photo is ready. It is as simple as that. In this chapter, we will find out how to build a customized photography drone using ArduPilot and some photography equipment. I forgot to mention one thing; there are a few rules for flying the drones. A few of them apply to photography drones, as they are heavier than some other drones. Some of the important rules are as follows:

- Your drone can not be flown over 400 feet, which is about 133 meters (don't worry; this is high enough for aerial photography. You can increase the limit by getting permission from the corresponding department in your country).
- Your drone must be always visible by you from your ground station. This is known as **Line of Sight (LOS)**.
- You cannot fly your drone near to any airports or no-fly-zone areas.
- You cannot fly your drone over a crowd. It is risky. If you are trying to take a group photo, then you should not fly your drone over the heads of your subjects, but take your photo from the front instead.
- Flying photography drones is a kind of threat to some people's privacy. So, I think you should respect that while flying your photography drones.
- Since drones got some negative publicity in the press, I must warn you to be careful with the laws and other privileges of the citizens.

Let's build our selfie or photography drone.

Requirements

The photography drone is almost similar to the other kind of drones, but with extra payload and a good camera. You can guess why the photography drone has to have extra payload: because it will carry a camera. If you use some kind of small weight digital camera, then your drone does not necessarily have to be able to have a good amount of payload. You can use your existing drone that we have already built with some customizations. The thing you need to remember is that the more you can control your drone and camera from the ground, the more you will be able to do good aerial photography. If you build a quadcopter as a photography drone, then whenever one of the motor fails, you will literally be doomed. If you build a hexacopter, then there is a little chance your drone and the camera will survive. So, the safest drone for photography is an octocopter. We will build an octocopter in this chapter.

You can also work with your quadcopter too; all you need is to modify the camera part. The following list shows the parts and hardware we will need to build an octocopter, as we will have to add a number of heavy things to the drone and the payload needs to be high. There is another reason to build the octocopter; that is that most of the drones in this book are quadcopters. So, I think we should also play with octocopters.

You will need the following components:

- 8 BLDC motors (I suggest SunnySky X4108S motors):

- 8 ESCs (you may use **Opto 25A** ESCs or **TBS Bulletproof 30A**):

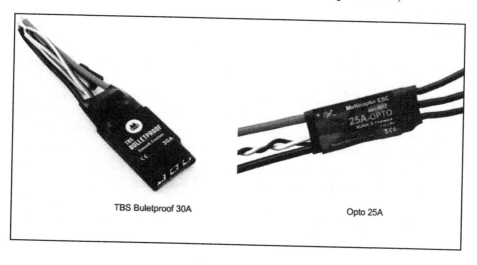

TBS Buletproof 30A   Opto 25A

- Flight controller (our ArduiPilot is enough here)
- Frame (you can build the frame by yourself or buy a HobbyKing X930 glass fiber frame (895 mm model preferred)) or a Tarot IRON MAN 100 carbon fiber octocopter frame
- 2 LiPo batteries (both 5,000 mAh)
- Radio
- Propellers (T-type 13x5.5 carbon fiber is suggested)
- Camera mount or gimbal
- Camera
- Other tools such as screwdrivers, soldering iron, glue gun, propeller balancer, jumpers, and so on.

Assembling the photography drone

Take out your frame and connect the parts together, as directed in the manual. However, I have a few suggestions to help you to carry out a better assembly of the frame:

1. Firstly, connect the motor mounted with the legs or wings or arms of the frame. Tighten them firmly, as they will carry and hold the most important equipment of the drone. Then, connect them to the base and, later, the other parts with firm connections.
2. Now, we will calibrate our ESCs. We will take the signal cable from an ESC (the motor is plugged into the ESC; careful, don't connect the propeller) and connect it to the throttle pins on the radio. Make sure the transmitter is turned on and the throttle is in the lowest position.
3. Now, plug the battery in to the ESC and you will hear a beep. Now, gradually increase the throttle from the transmitter. Your motor will start spinning at any position. This is because the ESC is not calibrated. So, you need to tell the ESC where the high point and the low point of the throttle are.
4. Disconnect the battery first. Increase the throttle of the transmitter to the highest position and power the ESC. Your ESC will now beep once and beep 3 times in every 4 seconds.
5. Now, move the throttle to the downmost position and you will hear the ESC beep as if it is ready and calibrated.

6. Now, you can increase the throttle of the transmitter and will see from lower to higher, the throttle will work.

7. Now, mount the motors, connect them to the ESCs, and then connect them to the ArduPilot, as in `Chapter 3`, *Preparing Your Drone for Flying*, changing the pins gradually.

8. Now, connect your GPS to the ArduPilot and calibrate it, as we did in `Chapter 3`, *Preparing Your Drone for Flying*.

9. Now, our drone is ready to fly. I would suggest you fly the drone for about 10-15 minutes before connecting the camera.

Connecting the camera

For a photography drone, connecting the camera and controlling the camera is one of the most important things. Your pictures and videos will be spoiled if you cannot adjust the camera and stabilize it properly. In our case, we will use a camera gimbal to hold the camera and move it from the ground.

Choosing a gimbal

The camera gimbal holds the camera for you and can move the camera direction according to your command. There are a number of camera gimbals out there. You can choose any type, depending on your demand and camera size and specification. If you want to use a DSLR camera, you should use a bigger gimbal and, if you use a point and shoot type camera or action camera, you may use small- or medium-sized gimbals. There are two types of gimbals, a brushless gimbal and a standard gimbal. The standard gimbal has servo motors and gears. If you use an FPV camera, then a standard gimbal with a 2-axis manual mount is the best option. The standard gimbal is not heavy; it is lightweight and not expensive. The best thing is you will not need an external controller board for your standard camera gimbal. The brushless gimbal is for professional aero photographers. It is smooth and can shoot videos or photos with better quality. The brushless gimbal will need an external controller board for your drone and the brushless gimbal is heavier than the standard gimbal. Choosing the best gimbal is one of the hard things for a photographer, as the stabilization of the image is a must for photoshoots. If you cannot control the camera from the ground, then using a gimbal is worthless.

The following picture shows a number of gimbals:

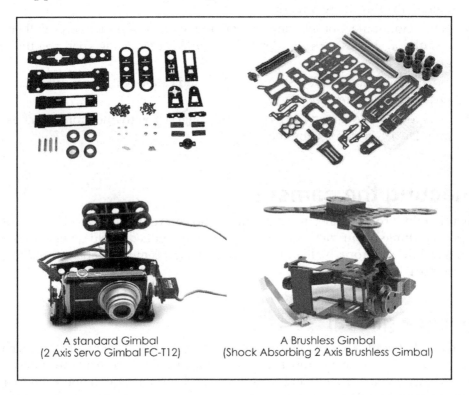

A standard Gimbal
(2 Axis Servo Gimbal FC-T12)

A Brushless Gimbal
(Shock Absorbing 2 Axis Brushless Gimbal)

After choosing your camera and the gimbal, the first thing is to mount the gimbal and the camera to the drone. Make sure the mount is firm, but not too hard, because it will make the camera shake while flying the drone. You may use the Styrofoam or rubber pieces that came with the gimbal to reduce the vibration and make the image stable.

Configuring the camera with the ArduPilot

Configuring the camera with the ArduPilot is easy. Remember the chapter where we made a package delivery drone? We can use the same trick here to control the gimbal servo while flying the drone or some other options of the ArduPilot.

Before going any further, let us learn a few things about the camera gimbal's Euler angels:

- **Tilt**: This moves the camera sloping position (range -90 degrees to +90 degrees), it is the motion (clockwise-anticlockwise) with the vertical axis
- **Roll**: This is a motion ranging from 0 degrees to 360 degrees parallel to the horizontal axis
- **Pan**: This is the same type motion of roll ranging from 0 degrees to 360 degrees but in the vertical axis
- **Shutter**: This is a switch that triggers a click or sends a signal

Firstly, we are going to use the standard gimbal. Basically, there are two servos in a standard gimbal. One is for pitch or tilt and another is for the roll. So, a standard gimbal gives you a two-dimensional motion with the camera view point.

Connection

Follow these steps to connect the camera to the ArduPilot:

1. Take the pitch servo's signal pin and connect it to the 11th pin of the ArduPilot (A11) and the roll signal to the 10th pin (A10). Make sure you connect only the signal (**S** pin) cable of the servos to the pin, not the other two pins (ground and the VCC).

2. The signal cables must be connected to the innermost pins of the A11 and A10 pins (two pins make a raw; see the following picture for clarification):

My suggestion is adding an extra battery for your gimbal's servos. If you want to connect your servo directly to the ArduPilot, your ArduPilot will not perform well, as the servos will draw power.

3. Now, connect your ArduPilot to your PC using wire or telemetry.
4. Go to the **Initial Setup** menu and, under **Optional Hardware**, you will find another option called **Camera Gimbal**. Click on this and you will see the following screen:

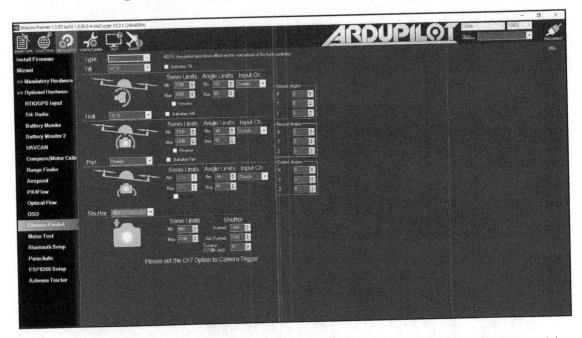

5. For the **Tilt**, change the pin to **RC11**; for the **Roll**, change the pin to **RC10**; and for **Shutter**, change it to CH7.

6. If you want to change the **Tilt** during the flight from the transmitter, you need to change the **Input Ch** of the **Tilt**. See the following screenshot:

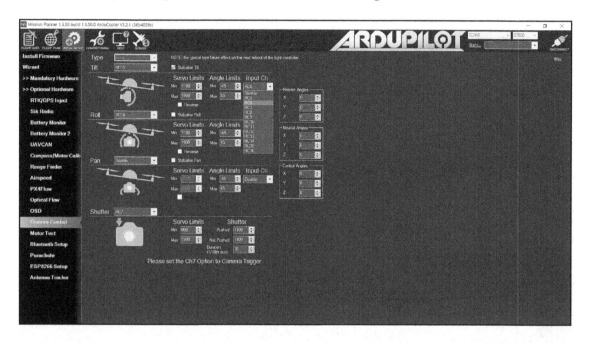

7. Now, you need to change an option in the **Configuration | Extended Tuning** page. Set **Ch6 Opt** to **None**, as in the following screenshot, and hit the **Write Params** button:

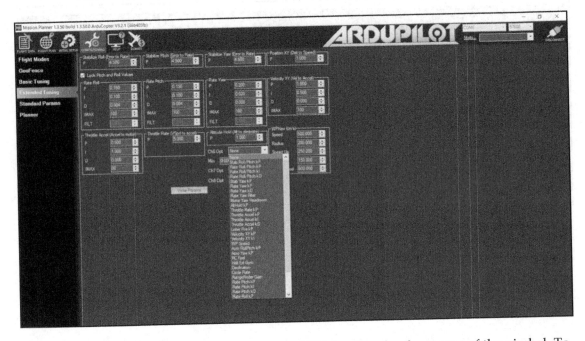

We need to align the minimum and maximum PWM values for the servos of the gimbal. To do that, we can tilt the frame of the gimbal to the leftmost position and from the transmitter, move the knob to the minimum position and start increasing, your servo will start to move at any time, then stop moving the knob. For the maximum calibration, move the **Tilt** to the rightmost position and do the same thing for the knob with the maximum position. Do the same thing for the pitch with the forward and backward motion. We also need to level the gimbal for better performance. To do that, you need to keep the gimbal frame level to the ground and set the **Camera Gimbal** option, the **Servo Limits**, and the **Angle Limits**. Change them as per the level of the frame.

Controlling the camera

Controlling the camera to take selfies or record video is easy. You can use the shutter pin we used before or the camera's mobile app for controlling the camera. My suggestion is to use the camera's app to take shots, because you will get a live preview of what you are shooting and it will be easy to control the camera shots. However, if you want to use the **Shutter** button manually from the transmitter then you can do this too. We have connected the RC7 pin for controlling a servo. You can use a servo or a receiver switch for your camera to manually trigger the shutter. To do that, you can buy a receiver controller on/off switch. You can use this switch for various purposes. Clicking the shutter of your camera is one of them. Manually triggering the camera is easy. It is usually done for point and shoot cameras. To do that, you need to update the firmware of your cameras. You can do this in many ways, but the easiest one will be discussed here.

Your **RECEIVER CONTROLLED ON/OFF SWITCH** may look like the following:

You can see five wires in the picture. The three wires together are, as usual, pins of the servo motor. Take out the signal cable (in this case, this is the yellow cable) and connect it to the RC7 pin of the ArduPilot. Then, connect the positive to one of the thick red wires. Take the camera's data cable and connect the other tick wire to the positive of the USB cable and the negative wire will be connected to the negative of the three connected wires. Then, an output of the positive and negative wire will go to the battery (an external battery is suggested for the camera).

To upgrade the camera firmware, you need to go to the camera's website and upgrade the firmware for the remote shutter option. In my case, the website is `http://chdk.wikia.com/wiki/CHDK`. I have downloaded it for a Canon point and shoot camera. You can also use action cameras for your drones. They are cheap and can be controlled remotely via mobile applications.

Flying and taking shots

Flying the photography drone is as you did before. My suggestion is to lock the altitude and fly parallel to the ground. If you use a camera remote controller or an app, then it is really easy to take the photo or record a video. However, if you use the switch, as we discussed, then you need to open and connect your drone to the mission planner via telemetry, go to the flight data, right click on the map, and then click the **Trigger Camera Now** option, which will trigger the **Camera Shutter** button and start recording or take a photo. You can do this when your drone is in a locked position and, using the timer, take a shot from above, which can be a selfie too. Let's try it. Let me know what happens and whether you like it or not. I have a few suggestions for taking good pictures and recording videos, using the drone.

Tips for better quality videos

It is really necessary to take care of the quality of the picture and the videos. So, if you are new to aerial photography with drones, then the following tips will be great for you:

- There is a famous effect called the Jello effect for aerial photography. This effect happens when the camera is vibrating and makes the image wobble unnaturally. This kind of effect mainly happens with cameras with a CMOS sensor, such as GoPros. To reduce the effect, you need to balance all the propellers (using a propeller balancer like this: `https://hobbyking.com/en_us/hobbykingtm-universal-propeller-balancer-for-t-style-and-std-propellers.html?___store=en_us`) and motor thrust. You can also use soft rubber, foam, or silicon plugs while mounting the camera to the drone.
- While moving the camera from the ground, you may have jerky camera movement. To reduce this, you can change the `RC_Feel` parameter to a lower number, such as 40 or 20.
- The digital stabilization system of the camera can also be a plus point for getting a better image or video.
- Always check the UAV forecast before flying a photography drone, because the weather plays a great role while taking photos and flying the drone.
- Since you are shooting from the sky, the light is sufficient. So, my suggestion is to use the lower ISO.
- If your camera has the option to take the footages in a raw format, then do it because you can edit them later.
- The shutter speed can be one sixth of a second or slower for properly exposed images.
- If your camera has an auto exposer option, then use it. It will make the images more beautiful.
- You can take some panoramic shots for higher quality photos.
- Be careful about the drone's flight time; always check your batteries before flying.
- While flying over the sea or rivers, be careful not to get too close so that water does not splash on the props or the camera. You can do this when you master the flying and controlling the gimbal.
- If the sun is too bright, use camera lens filters for natural quality images.
- Always take images as bird's eye views and stick to the lines, such as roads or lines of trees and so on.
- You may ask which is better, 16:9 or 4:3 format? My suggestion is try both yourself. I use a 16:9 format a lot, because of the image size. You can try any of the formats, depending on your camera and the environment.

- Always check your compass is calibrated. Otherwise, you cannot move your drone to the perfect position. Check the previews on your screen if you have this option available on your camera via Wi-Fi.
- Always mind the privacy of people and wildlife.
- My personal suggestion for a stable picture is to hold the altitude and take some continuous shots from forward and backward. Then, choose one.
- Try to follow the shapes or natural phenomenon or man-made structures from the sky and take pictures.

Have you thought about the fact that moving the gimbal is kind of hard? You can use an ESP8266 to remotely control the Gimbal's servo. In fact, you can make a camera gimbal of your own, too. Let's see how you can control a two-axis camera gimbal using the ESP8266.

Controlling the camera gimbal using ESP8266

In this section, we will make a custom gimbal with two-servo motors that can be controlled remotely. You need to buy a Servo bracket to install the servos. You can buy a cheap one like
this: `https://www.aliexpress.com/item/Servo-bracket-PT-Pan-Tilt-Camera-Platform-Anti-Vibration-Camera-Mount-for-Aircraft-FPV-dedicated-nylon/32697306736.html`.
You will need the following things:

- ESP8266 or NodeMCU
- Two-servo motors (SG90 mini gear micro servo preferred)
- 5V power supply
- Smart phone
- Router (for Wi-Fi connection)

Let's see how this is done:

1. Firstly, attach the servos to the bracket. Connect the servos to the ESP8266, as follows:

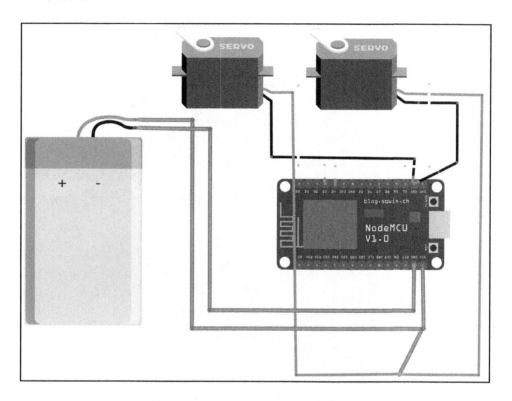

2. From the diagram, you can see that the servos are connected to the GPIO pins of the ESP8266. GPIO 0 and GPIO 2 or D3 and D4, respectively. Now you need to write code for our ESP8266 but, before that, open your Blynk app and create a **New Project**:

3. Give your project a name and from **Choose Device**, select **NodeMCU** or **ESP8266**, whichever you use for your gimbal. Hit **Create Project**. Remember the authentication code of the project. The code will also be sent to your email.

4. Next, swipe right to get the **Widget Box** and choose **Slider**:

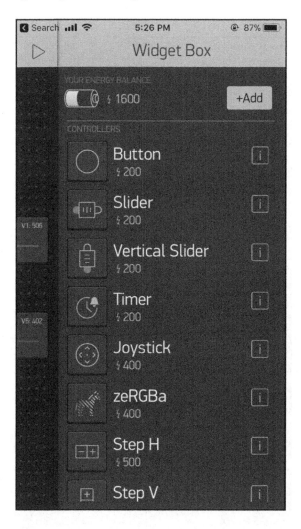

5. Give your slider a name. I gave `Servo 1` and `Servo 2` for the two sliders we need:

6. Select a **Virtual** pin for each of the sliders. I chose **V1** and **V6**:

7. Your final look of the project will look like the following screenshot. You may change the color from the slider properties:

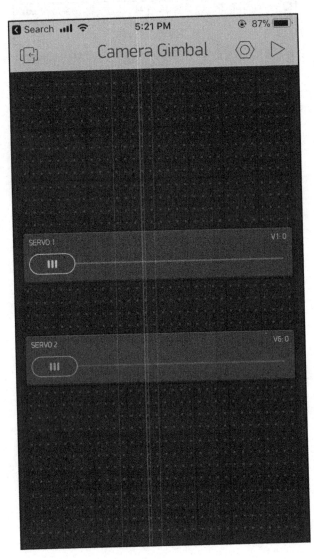

Let's begin our coding to control the gimbal:

1. Fire up your Arduino IDE and add the following lines at the top of the sketch:

```
#define BLYNK_PRINT Serial
#include <SPI.h>
#include <BlynkSimpleEsp8266.h>
#include <Servo.h>
#include <ESP8266WiFi.h>
```

2. You need to install the ESP8266 libraries to do that.

3. Now, declare the authentication code you got for your project and the Wi-Fi name and password for the connection, as follows:

```
char auth[] = "***********";
char ssid[] = "***********";
char pass[] = "***********";
```

4. Then, declare our servos:

```
Servo s1, s2;
```

5. Inside the `void setup()`, we need to start the Blynk and then attach the servo pins:

```
Serial.begin(9600);
Blynk.begin(auth, ssid, pass);
s1.attach(0);
s2.attach(2);
```

6. Then, assign the virtual pins of the Blynk, as follows:

```
BLYNK_WRITE(V1)
  {
    s1.write(param.asInt());
  }
BLYNK_WRITE(V6)
  {
    s2.write(param.asInt());
  }
```

7. Then in the `void loop()` function, run the Blynk:

   ```
   Blynk.run();
   ```

   The full source code can be found here:
   `https://github.com/SOFTowaha/Selfie-Drone/blob/master/blynkCode.in`
   `o.`

8. Now, verify and upload the code after connecting the NodeMCU to the computer.

9. From your Blynk application, run the project. You will see your sliders, as follows:

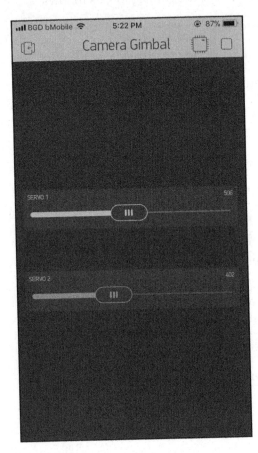

10. Now, if you move your sliders from left to right, you will see your servos will move **0-180** degrees.

You may get some resonances. So, I would suggest you use an LM1117 voltage regulator between the NodeMCU and the battery or the power supply. Now, I have some home work for you. I want you to make a switch from the Blynk and trigger the camera you will use in the drone using Blynk application.

Summary

In this chapter, we have learned how we can build and configure our photography drone. We have also learned some tips of aerial photography and some tricks with the camera movements. We made our custom camera gimbal to remotely control the camera. I hope you will build a photography drone and enjoy it. In Chapter 7, *Building Prototype Drones – Gliding Drones*, we will learn about different types of drone. To find out what type of drone we will be building, just go to Chapter 7, *Building Prototype Drones – Gliding Drones*, and see if you can build one for yourself.

7

Building Prototype Drones – Gliding Drones

In this chapter, we will make an unusual type of drone, a gliding drone. You may have seen such planes; they just glide in the air and go to their destination. In this chapter, we will make drones like such planes, and learn the physics behind the gliding drones or the fixed wing drones. We will also know the aerodynamics of the flying of the fixed-wings. So, let's begin our chapter with an introduction to the gliding drone and the aerodynamics of the gliding drone.

What is a glider?

Have you ever made a paper plane? Well, a paper plane is an example of a glider. A glider does not depend on engines; it depends on aerodynamics and the physics of flying, like a bird hovering in the air without moving its wings. The gliding drone is little bit more complicated than the usual copters. The glider has to follow the winds and the weather. The direction of the wind is but one of many variables. The following image shows a glider (DG Flugzeugbau DG-800).

Glider drones are also known as fixed wing drones:

There are three main surfaces of a glider. They are:

- Wing
- Stabilizer
- Vertical fin

The wing provides the lifting of the glider. For the wing, the glider glides and stables itself by means of the stabilizer. In some gliders, stabilizers are not available. There are two things related to the wing that should be known; wing area and wing loading.

The wing area is the product of the wing length, or wing span, and the chord or the width, of wing.

So, *Wing Area = Wing Span x Wing Chord.*

And the wing loading is the ratio of the weight of the wing and the wing area.

So, *Wing Loading = Weight/Wing Area*.

Let's see an example. Say a wing is 10 feet long, the chord of wing is 2 feet and the weight of the wing is 1 kg.

Firstly, we need to convert the unit from feet to inch and kg to g:

- 10 feet = 120 inch
- 2 feet = 24 inch
- 1 kg = 1000 gm

So the *Wing Area = 120 x 24 = 2880 square inch* and *Wing Loading = 1000/2880 = 0.3472 gm/sq. inch.*

For a small glider, the wing loading is better if it is around 0.33 gm/sq inch, as seen from the payload calculation.

Just a short note; wing area is denoted by S as it is also called wing surface area (in square feet or square inches).

We will now learn a few other things related to the glider. As you can guess, the glider follows Newton's 3rd Law of Motion, which is that for every action there is an opposite and equal reaction. For the glider, the air that is deflected downwards (action) produces an upward force (reaction); that's why a torque is created, and hence the glider floats for as long as the forces are equal and not destroyed by the friction of the air or other things. As we have learned about the wing construction above, the design takes advantage of certain laws of physics that produce the two actions from the air mass below the wing. Therefore, negative pressure will apply a lifting action to the glider due to the lowered pressure above the wing.

Now, we will learn the following concepts in relation to the glider. These may seem confusing, but if you really want to know the beauty of aerodynamics with regards to a glider, you should know these:

- Lift
- Drag
- Airfoil and its type
- Incident and decalage angle
- Three axis motion (pitch, roll, and yaw)
- Thrust

- Aspect ratio and glide ratio
- Glide or dive, descent and gliding angle
- Climb
- Centre of pressure
- Pitching moment
- Load factors
- Angle of attack

Lift

For a glider, the lift is the opposite downward force of the gravity (named, weight), which is produced by the dynamic effects of the surrounding airstream acting on the wings of the glider. See the following diagram to get the idea:

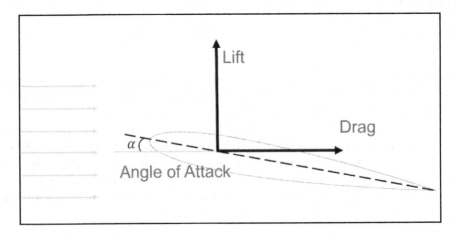

Lift is perpendicular to the flight direction of the glider. The coefficient of the lift is a dimensionless number that is the ratio of the lift pressure and area of the wing. So, the lift directly depends on the airfoil of the glider. There is an equation for finding out the lift of a glider. If L is the lift, then:

$$L = C_L V^2 \frac{\rho}{2} S$$

where C_L is the coefficient of the lift, V is the velocity of the glider, r is the density of the air, and S is wing area. The lift can be calculated easily if we know the glide angle:

$$\text{Lift} = \text{Weight} \times \text{Cosine of the Glide Angle.}$$

Drag

Drag is nothing but a force. It opposes the glider's motion through the air. Drag is produced by almost every part of the glider. As it is generated by the interaction and contact of a solid body or liquid (air or water or gas), it can be called a mechanical force.

Drag is expressed by the following formula:

$$\text{Drag} = \text{Weight of the Glider} \times \text{Sine of the Glide Angle.}$$

Drag comes in a few types, such as parasites drag, skin friction drag, induced drag, interference drag, total drag, form drag, and so on:

- **Parasite drag:** Parasite drag is the resistance of the air to the glider moving through the air. The drag on the wing is very low if we consider a standalone wing, but when calculated for the whole glider, the drag is significant. My idea from the calculation shows that if the speed of the glider is doubled, the parasite drag is increased four times over. Parasite drag comes in three types:
  - **Skin friction drag**: Skin friction drag is caused by the roughness of the glider's body or the outer surface. Even though the surface is smooth, there is skin friction drag; air is a viscous fluid, so the stationary layer of the air hits the wing of the glider and creates skin friction drag.
  - **Form drag**: Form drag is caused by the shape of the wing. You can imagine when a glider glides through the air, the air also moves out of that space, creating a friction against the body of the glider. Actually, form drag is created by the turbulent wake of the glider, which is caused by the separation of the airflow from the surface of the glider.
  - **Interference drag**: Interference drag occurs when the flow of air meets and interacts after passing the glider, or while colliding with the glider body.

There is another type of drag, known as induced drag. **Induced drag** is generated for the lift. To define induced drag, we can say that when the wing of the glider is driven through the air to create the pressure difference, induced drag is created.

So, you can guess what the total drag is. Yes, the sum of the parasite drag and the induced drag is known as the total drag.

Airfoil and its type

Normally, airfoil is nothing but the wing shape of the glider. When we use it, we mean the cross-sectional shape of the wing. Airfoil plays a great role in flying the glider. The leading edge is the front edge of the wing, the trailing edge is the back edge of the wing, the chord line is the connecting line from the leading edge to the trailing edge, the camber line is almost the chord line but it equidistant from the upper and the lower surfaces of the glider, and the camber is the asymmetry between the top and bottom curves of an airfoil (in a vertical cross section).

In the following figure, you can see a few types of airfoil:

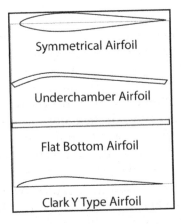

The speed and the gliding varies from airfoil to airfoil. To me, the best airfoil type is **Clark Y type Airfoil**, because the drag and the lift are good for that type of airfoil.

Incident and decalage angle

The incident angle is the angle between the chord line and the longitudinal axis. The decalage angle is the angle difference between the upper and lower wings of the glider.

See the following diagram for clarification:

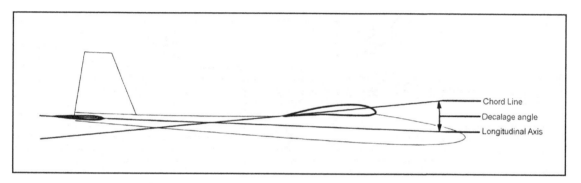

Three axis motion (roll, pitch, and yaw)

We already know these types of motion from `Chapter 6`, *Building a Drone to Take Selfies and Record Videos*, but we will use the glider to recap them. Roll is the motion along the longitudinal axis, pitch is the motion along the lateral axis, and yaw is the motion along the vertical axis.

The following image demonstrates the direction of all three motions:

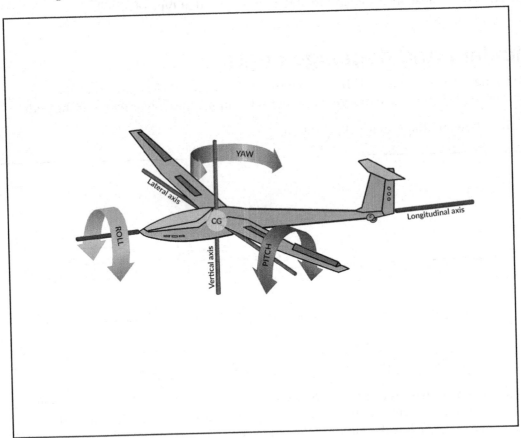

Thrust

For our glider drone, we will use a motor in front of the glider. It will be placed on the nose/head of the glider, pointing forwards. The thrust is the forward force that propels the glider through the air. If there is no motor on the glider (like with a paper plane), the thrust will be the conversion of the kinetic energy and the potential energy.

The mathematical expression for thrust is:

$$T = D + (W \times sinC)$$

Here, T is thrust, W is the weight of the glider, D is the drag and $sinC$ of the is the sine angle of the climb.

There is a beautiful relation among them:

Thrust + Lift = Drag + Weight

We will discuss this while we study the mechanics of glide flying.

Aspect ratio and glide ratio

Aspect ratio is calculated by dividing the wing span or the wing area by the average length of the chord. The glider wings usually have the highest AR:

$$AR = \frac{S}{C}$$

S is the wing area and C is the average chord length.

The **Glide Ratio (GR)** is defined as follows:

$$GR = \frac{Lift}{Drag} : 1$$

$$\text{or} \quad GR = \frac{Velocity\,of\,air}{The\,rate\,of\,Sink} : 1$$

From the first relation, we can understand that minimizing the *Drag* is very important. As the *Drag* varies with the speed of the air, the second relation is true. Remember that, for the second relation, the air speed and the sink rate have to be in the same unit.

Glide or dive and descent, gliding angle

When a glider does not maintain altitude, the phenomenon is called descending or diving. If the glider does not generate enough lift for its own weight, then the glider will fly down towards the ground. In this situation, the nose of the glider will be pointed downwards. So, with the ground, the nose of the glider creates an angle that is known as the gliding angle.

In other words, the angle between the plane of the horizon and the path of the glider is known as the gliding angle. The simplest equation for the **Gliding Angle (GA)** is as follows:

$$GA = (H/D) \times A$$

Where H is the height from the ground, D is the plane length and A is arctangle.

Climb

Do you remember the lift? When the lift is greater than the weight of the glider, the nose of the glider moves (pitches) upwards. Then, when the thrust is created using the pops connected to the glider, it pulls the glider to an increasingly steep angle. The amount of lift actually decreases as more force comes from the pull of the upwards. When the glider is completely vertical in the hover position, there is no lift on the wing of the glider. So, the climb is nothing but the front/nose of the glider moving upwards. The angle is also known as the **Angle of Attack (AOA)**.

Center of pressure

Center of pressure is the point where the total sum of the pressure acts on a body, causing a force to act through that point. The total force vector acting at the center of pressure is the value of the integrated vectorial pressure field.

Pitching moment

The force acting vertically on the airfoil to stabilize the glider is known as the pitching moment.

Load factor

Any kind of force applied to the glider to deflect the flight direction produces a stress in the glider structure. The amount of force is called the load factor.

Angle of attack

The angle between the wind and the wing is known as the angle of attack. If the angle of attack increases, the lift is generated.

Now that we have covered a basic introduction to aerodynamics, let's learn how the glider flies.

How a glider glides

We know about gravity, the downward attraction force for bodies that have mass. We have learned about lift, thrust, and drag. Basically, these four types of aerodynamic forces are what fly a glider drone. In a short definition, the gravity is an upward force, the thrust is the forward force, the drag is the backward force, and the lift is an upward force.

To fly the glider, the thrust must be greater than the drag and the lift must be greater than the gravity. The easiest option is to cancel the opposite forces.

The take-off and climbs must take place to fly the glider.

All the forces should be balanced, otherwise the glider will fall apart. The wing can generate lift, as we have studied before. The air approaches the wing and then splits at the leading edge of the wing and meets again at the trailing edge; therefore, the air must go faster over the top of the wing as this distance is larger. For a working glider, I suggest the following measurements:

- **Wing span**: 50-60 cm
- **Aspect ratio**: 9-10
- **Angle of attack**: 3-4 degree

Let's build our own glider drone

In this section we will build our own glider. Before going any further, let's see what the requirements are.

Firstly, we need to select a design for the glider. There are a number of designs you can choose. Depending on the wing shape, there are four types of gliders:

- Elliptical wing
- Rectangular wing
- Tapered wing
- Swept-forward wing

In this chapter, we are going to choose the rectangle-shaped wing. The other necessary equipment is as follows:

- Propellers
- ESCs
- Motors
- Battery
- ArduPilot
- Servos
- RC receiver and transmitter
- Some carbon fiber tubes
- Some steel wires
- Some nylon pushrods

To begin with, make the body; we will install the other parts after. If you have a 3D printer, you can print the parts of the body and install them. You can also use airfoil for the wing and body design. To make the frame you will need airfoil, a glue gun, a knife, blades, and measurement tools.

Take a board of the airfoil and measure 6-7 inches from the bottom. Score the paper as shown in the following picture:

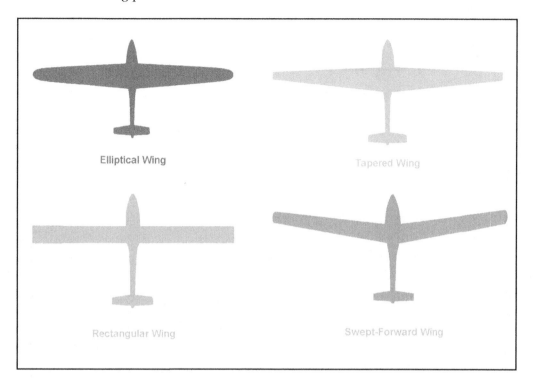

Peel off the airfoil paper from the bottom side and fold it inward, trying to bend it like a curve. Now cut three pieces, sliced one-inch in length, and glue them inside the structure you just made. Add another one-inch slice on the top of the innermost slice and cure the structure. Glue them using the glue gun. You can use one slice if you want a lighter wing. To make it strong, you can use PVC slices instead of the airfoil inside:

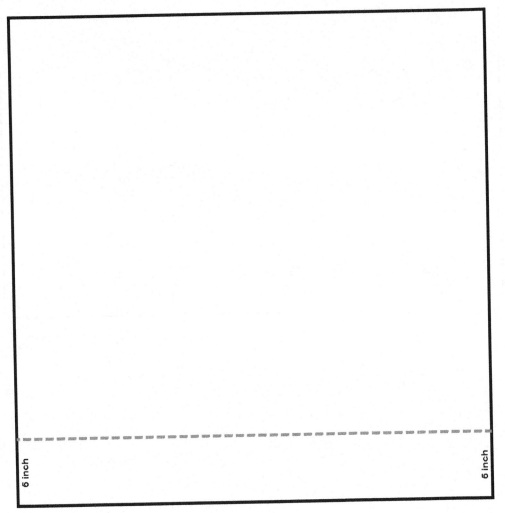

You have just made one side of the wing. Make another piece like this and join them together with a few more slices of the airfoil. After making the wing, you need to make a passage in the center of the wing for the wiring (see the following diagram; **C** is the passage). Also, for the servo motor installation, cut the paper of the airfoil on **A** and **B**:

The body can be made by starting with a cuboid with the airfoil, with the height as the long side. In the front of the cuboid, for motor mounting, add a strong PVC or steel board. Also, make a passage in the center for wiring. For the tail of the glider, follow the same procedure with the calculations we have learned before. For easy calculations of the frame, you can use this site: http://chrusion.com/BJ7/SuperCalc7.html. Now, observe the following picture, which shows you where to add the components:

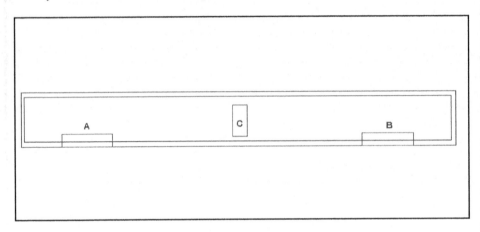

The setup procedure would be as follows:

1. Mount the motor in front of the glider
2. Add the propeller to the motor
3. Connect ESC to the motor
4. Connect ESC and servos to ArduPilot
5. For the aileron, set pin 1
6. For the elevator, set pin 2
7. For the throttle, set pin 3
8. For the rudder, set pin 4
9. Add the radio, on the proper channels
10. Connect ArduPilot to the mission planner using USB
11. Select **Proper COM** port and Click on **Connect**
12. Go to **Initial Setup** | **Install Firmware**
13. Select **ArduPlane** and click **OK**
14. You will be asked if you want to install the firmware
15. Install the firmware
16. After installing the firmware, test it by moving ArduPilot

17. Connect the power to the glider
18. Take the glider outside
19. Arm your remote
20. The propeller should start moving if you give it throttle
21. Throw the glider forward, as we do not have landing gear installed
22. Control it from your remote

The glider will have throttle (the BLDC motor), aileron (the servos installed on the wing), an elevator (servos installed on the tail), and a rudder (servo installed on the top side of the tail). See the following diagram for clarification:

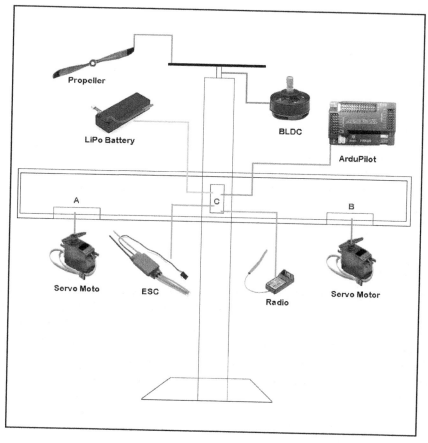

The following configuration is a tweak for the pin setup:

- **Channel 1**: Left aileron
- **Channel 2**: Right aileron
- **Channel 3**: Throttle (ESC)

For the receiver and ArduPilot:

Receiver	ArduPilot
Pin 1	Pin 1
Pin 2	Pin 2
Pin 3	Pin 3
Pin 4	Pin 4
Pin 5	Pin 5
Pin 6	Pin 6
Pin 7	Pin 7
Pin 8	Pin 8

You can add the GPS, air speed sensor, and some other sensors for more accurate location and environment data.

Summary

In this chapter, we have learned how a gliding drone flies, and a number of things about aerodynamics. I hope you will make a glider drone and share your experience with me. We also learned how you can make airfoil glider wings, add the components to the body of the glider, and how to set up ArduPilot. In Chapter 8, *Building Prototype Drones – Racing Drone*, we will make another type of drone known as a racing drone. The racing drone will be fun if you like competition with your friends. So, let's begin making the racing drone.

8

Building Prototype Drones – Racing Drones

No one remembers the runners up in any game. Drone racing is becoming a popular game in the world. The **First Person View** (**FPV**) of drone racing is the most popular. In FPV racing, only the pilot can see what the drone sees. The pilot wears head mounted displays, where he/she can see the things from the camera installed on the drone and controls the drone with the remote. In the competitions, there is a defined path given with a number of obstacles and zigzag routes. The pilots are meant to fly the drone through the path and complete the set course as quickly as possible. Feeling excited? Well, in this chapter, we will be building a racing drone. And, at the end of the chapter, we will know a few rules and regulations regarding the racing drones. Let's begin with the introduction of the racing drone.

Racing drones

Any drone can be used for racing. But there is some criteria set by the FPV drone racing leagues that needs to fulfilled by the drone we will race with. The basic requirements of a racing drone are as follows:

- They should be small and lightweight.
- They should be crash proof as they may hit a lot of obstacles.
- They should have a real-time camera to see the tracks.
- The motors used in racing drones are set in an H pattern to thrust the drone forward, not upward.
- The communication between the drone and the remote must be good; otherwise, you can guess what will happen.

- Since the drones are competing to finish the race, they must be faster than other drones.
- For the racing drone, the main goal is controlling the drone and finishing the path as quickly as possible. So, the less number of processes we will run on the brain of the drone, the faster it will run.
- They should have first person view camera googles with video streamed from the drone.
- They should be repairable.

So, now you can guess what kind of drone we will be building in this chapter. Most of the racing drones are copters. We will build a quadcopter in this chapter with the highest speed and the most durability. Let's collect the equipment first. We can use our existing quadcopter with a few tweaks or we can rebuild a fresh drone for racing. Let's see what our equipment list will be:

- A frame (I prefer a lightweight frame such as a Diatone Beta110):

- Four BLDC motors (I like the cheap model Kingkong 2204-2300 KV):

- Four ESCs (hobbywing X rotor 250 size ESC 10 amp preferred):

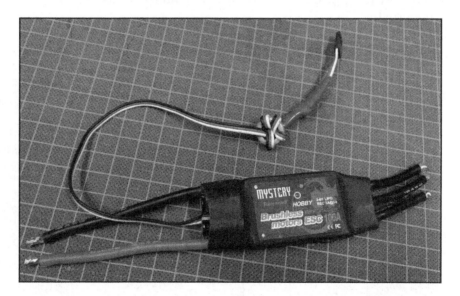

- Four propellers (two CW and two CCW), 5-inch ones are preferred (you can buy the cheap German Carbon/Nylon 5030):

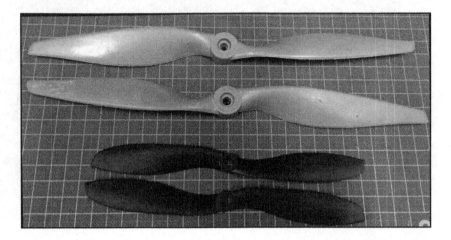

- A battery (a lightweight battery such as a multistar racer series 2,200 mAh are preferred):

- A flight controller (a light flight controller is preferred but our ArduPilot will do the trick)

- GPS (Walkera QR X350 is lightweight and preferred):

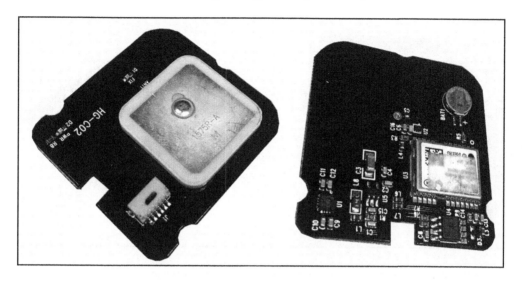

- Telemetry modules and radio
- An FPV camera (mini CMOS 600 TVL FPV camera 505 M) and a Mini OSD to APM (as we are using ArduPilot):

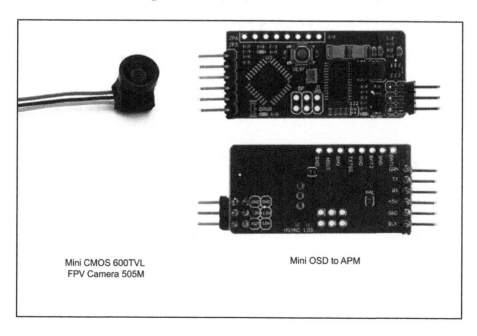

Mini CMOS 600TVL
FPV Camera 505M

Mini OSD to APM

- An FTDI basic adapter:

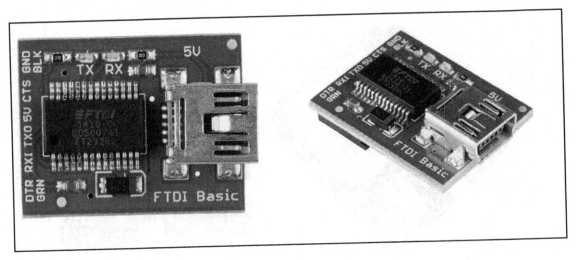

- Other tools such as a battery checker and FPV antenna

Assembling the racing drone

We already built a number of working drones in the last seven chapters, so it won't take much time to assemble the racing drone, because assembling the racing drone is almost similar to the other drones. The only thing different you need to take care of here is adding the FPV camera connection. Since we are using the ArduPilot, it is a bit complicated. But you can follow the instructions and I'm sure you will configure it in no time. Before adding the FPV camera, I would suggest you assemble the drone and fly it for a few minutes.

Connecting the FPV camera

We will connect the OSD to the ArduPilot telemetry port and we will connect the camera and the video transmitter.

We need to download software for the FPV camera. You just plug the FTDI Basic to the OSD mini and you are ready to connect to the USB cable. The connection between the FTDI basic and the MinimOSD would be as follows:

MInimOSD	FTDI basic
Rx	Tx
Tx	Rx
GND	GND
VCC	VCC

For more clarification, refer to the following screenshot. The other end of the USB cable will go to the computer for flashing a firmware to the OSD. There are a number of software tools available for the OSD. We will work with the easiest open source firmware called **arducam-osd**. To get this, go to the link `https://code.google.com/archive/p/arducam-osd/` and click on the **HERE** link:

Refer to the following steps:

1. Go to the **Downloads** option from the left menu. You will find a .hex file and a .zip file. Download both of them. Open the OSD_Config.exe file from a Windows machine and plug in the other end of the USB cable to your PC, which you just plugged into the FTDI basic.

2. You will see the following screen:

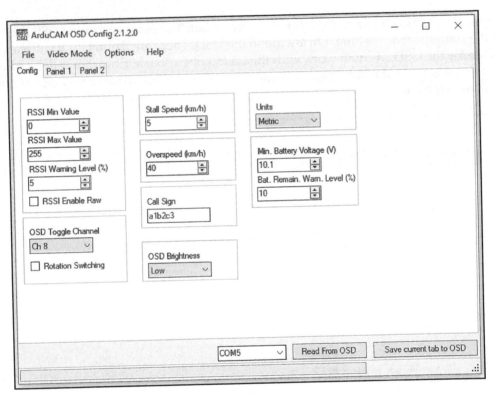

3. Once you connect the OSD via the FTDI basic to your PC, select the correct COM port from the software you just opened.

4. Then go to **Option | Update Firmware** and select the .hex file we downloaded. And once you select the file, your OSD's firmware will be automatically updated. You will get a Done message after the firmware is uploaded.

5. Now, you need to update the character set of the OSD. To do this, go to **Option | UpdateCharSet**. Select the OSD_Charset.mcm file from the extracted .zip file we downloaded. After the character set uploading is done, you will get another Done message.

6. Now, we will change some parameters on the **Config** panel as follows:
   - **Stall Speed** (mph) to at least 65-75 km/h
   - **Overspeed** (mph) to 40-45 km/h, min
   - **Min. Battery Voltage** (V) to 10.5 as we will be using our 3 cell 2,200 mAh battery for the racing drone.
   - **Bat. Remain. Wan. Level (%)** to 10-15
7. And hit the **Save current tab to OSD** button.
8. Now, go to **Panel 1** and select the things you will need on the video from the left side. Just click on the tick and the preview screen on the right side will change according to your selection.
9. And after selecting the options you need, click on the **Save current tab to OSD** button. Now, go to **Panel 2** and click on the **Save current tab to OSD** button again.
10. We have successfully updated our OSD firmware; now we need to connect the OSD to the camera, video transmitter, and the ArduPilot.

Connect the OSD to the telemetry pins directly. The pin configuration is as follows:

OSD pin	Telemetry pin
GND	GND
+5V	+5V
Tx	Tx
Rx	Rx

Refer to the following circuit diagram for connecting all the components:

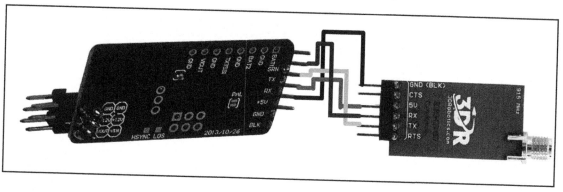

The last thing is powering up the drone and connecting the other telemetry to the PC/smart phone and receive the information there.

Hence, our racing drone is ready. Now, go out and join some drone racing communities and start racing. Don't worry if you break anything. It is very common for the first time. Just play with your racing drone; you will definitely be able to get lots of fun out of it.

In this section, we will learn how we can make an object able to avoid obstacles using a sensors and our favorite ESP8266.

Avoiding obstacles using ESP8266

We will use a sensor to sense any object in front of it. We will use an ultrasonic sensor (HC-SR04 preferred). The intensity of the sensor will be shown by our Blynk app. So, let's start with the connection.

Connect the D1 and D2 to the Tring and Echo pins respectively. Since the sensor needs a 5V power supply, we will use an external battery to power it up. We will also use the same battery to power the NodeMCU after uploading the code. The pinout is as follows:

HC-SR04	NodeMCU
Trig	D1
Echo	D2
GND	GND
VCC	Vin

Refer to the following circuit diagram for clarification:

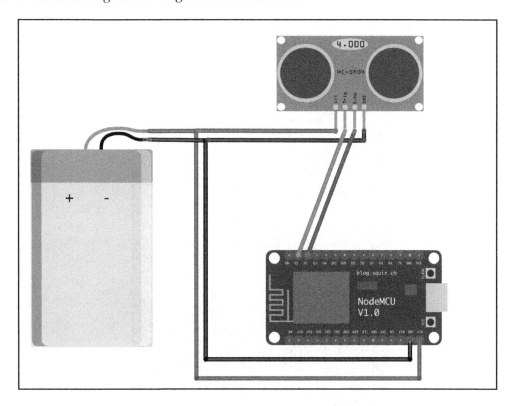

Refer to the following steps:

1. Now, we open the Blynk app and create a project with the following settings:

2. From the widgets, select **Gauge**. From the properties of the gauge, select a **Virtual** pin (I choose **V1**). Your Blynk part is done:

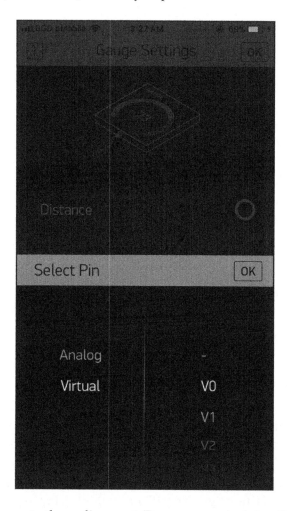

3. Now, let's move to the coding part. Fire up your Arduino IDE and add the following libraries:

```
#include <ESP8266WiFi.h>
#include <BlynkSimpleEsp8266.h>
```

4. Now, declare three character arrays for our Wi-Fi SSID, password, and the authentication code of the Blynk project we just created:

```
char auth[] = "**********";
char ssid[] = "**********";
char pass[] = "**********";
```

5. Inside the `void setup()` function, write the following code:

```
Blynk.begin(auth, ssid, pass); //This will start the Blynk with
proper credentials
pinMode(4, OUTPUT); //for trigger in D1
pinMode(5, INPUT); //for echo in D2
```

6. After declaring two long variables in the `void loop()` function as the distance and the time, we will set the `trigger` to LOW first. After a very short delay, we will make it HIGH and then again make it LOW:

```
digitalWrite(4, LOW); //for trigger
delayMicroseconds(2);
digitalWrite(4, HIGH);
delayMicroseconds(10);
digitalWrite(4, LOW);
```

7. Now, we will get the `duration` from the echo and from the duration using mathematical formula, we will find the `distance`:

```
duration = pulseIn(5, HIGH); //for echo
distance = (duration / 2) / 29.1;
```

8. After finding the distance, we need to print it through the virtual pin V0:

```
Blynk.virtualWrite(V0, distance);
```

9. Since the previous code will be executed over and over again as they are in the `void loop()` function, we will add a short delay to get the proper distance. And, finally, run the Blynk:

```
delay(200);
Blynk.run();
```

The full source code can be found at: (`https://github.com/SOFTowaha/RacingDrone/blob/master/AvoidObstacle.ino`).

Let's upload the code and start the Blynk app. Now, run the project and you will see that the gauge will show you the distance of the obstacle from it. You can use this short tweak to do anything you want to make them avoid obstacles.

Summary

In this chapter, we have learned how we can construct a racing drone and connect the first person view camera using our existing ArduPilot. The process might look a bit complicated, but when you see the real-time video from your drone with the CMOS camera to your screen, all your hard work will pay off. We also learned a simple ESP8266 tweak to make the drone avoid any obstacles and see the data from a mobile application.

In Chapter 9, *Maintaining and Troubleshooting Your Drone*, we will learn a number of things regarding drone troubleshooting and maintenance. So, if you want to be a professional drone pilot, then Chapter 9, *Maintaining and Troubleshooting Your Drone* is really necessary for you.

9

Maintaining and Troubleshooting Your Drone

In the last eight chapters, we have built a number of drones for different types of usage. But if you do not know how you can troubleshoot your own drone, that is a shame. You also have to know how to maintain your drone whether you do not fly it for a long time or fly regularly. So, let's begin the chapter with some maintenance tips for the drone.

Safety of the drone

Always look carefully at your drone after every flight to check whether there is any damage. Inspect the outer shell and the propellers carefully. If you see any damaged component, do not hesitate to change or repair it. Before every flight, check the battery stage and the propellers' condition. Never fly your drone if your props are not firmly connected or motors are not mounted properly. Remove them if there is any dust or dirt on the outer shell of the drone or the gimbal, because not doing so might cause the drone's component to have a hardware failure.

Be careful about the battery

The battery of the drone is one of the most important things. Without the battery, you cannot even power the drone. So taking care of the battery is a must. Since we use a LiPo battery for our drone, there are some things you should know in order to save the battery life. Always use the fully charged battery in your drone while flying. If you wish to keep the battery idle for a long time, charge it to 40 to 65 % and store it in a dry location at a proper temperature, as specified in the battery manual.

Do not allow the battery to have contact with any kind of liquid, as it may short circuit and then reduce the battery life. Always look at the battery monitor while flying the drone. If you see your battery is draining too fast, then land your drone immediately and inspect all the connections and allow the battery to cool down. You can also add the FS_BATT_VOLTAGE and FS_BATT_MAH to enable battery failsafe. There are some temperature limits within which you should use the battery. It varies from company to company. So, refer to the battery manual before using the battery in too high a temperature. You must not charge the battery right after a flight, because the battery becomes hot while discharging, and if you charge it while it is hot, the lifetime will be reduced. In the manual, you will also find out at what temperature you can charge the battery. Use a battery voltage checker for checking that each cell of the battery is getting properly charged. You can fully discharge and then charge your battery fully every 2-3 months to maintain a good battery cycle. This will increase the LiPo battery's lifetime.

Storage of the drone

If you want to store your drone, always use a safe box or briefcase with silica gel for creating a moisture-free environment for the components. You need to store your drone in a cool, dry, and non-magnetic place. If you want to keep your drone unused for more than three months, then store it at room temperature, which is around 25 degrees centigrade. You can remove the propellers, and disconnect the telemetry and radio if you want to store the drone for a long time.

Carrying a drone

Store the battery in a separate case while carrying it. Make sure the battery case does not have any metal plates. Detach the camera gimbal while carrying the drone. You can recalibrate the compass if you are travelling for a long time. You should remove your propellers to carry the drone safely.

Before and after flight safety

Turn on the remote controller before you turn on the drone. It will make sure that the drone is always under control. After the flight, turn off the drone first and then switch off the remote controller. Attach the gimbal clamp after a flight.

Respect the law and privacy

You must not do anything with your drone that is illegal. Always try to know the law about flying the drone before flying a drone in any place. If necessary, request the required permission. Respect other people's privacy. Drones may make a sound and have a camera installed on them, so, while flying, respect other people's privacy and consider whether you may be annoying them. Drones have received negative publicity from the press, so be careful about this.

Troubleshooting your drone

Your drone may have some problems when you fly it regularly or if you have just started piloting a drone. This can be because of maintenance or accidents. So, we need to troubleshoot and fly our drone safely. In this section, we will look at a few common troubleshooting tips.

My drone tries to flip or flip when I turn it on

This problem may occur for several reasons. Check if you calibrated your ESCs. Are your propellers balanced? Have you configured the radio properly? Are your ArduPilot's sensors working properly? Have you checked all the wire connection? Have you calibrated the drone frame? Have you added the wrong propellers to the wrong motors (for example, clockwise propellers to anticlockwise motors)? I hope you can solve the problem now.

My motors spin but the drone does not fly or take off

This happens because the motors are not giving enough thrust to take off the drone. From the parameter list of the Mission Planner, change THR_MAX . Make sure it is in between 800 and 1000. If THR_MAX is 800 and still the drone does not take off, change the parameter to above 800 and try flying again.

The drone moves in any direction

The drone moves in any direction even though the stick of the transmitter is cantered. To solve the problem, you must match the RC channel's 1 and 2 values to the PWM values displayed on the Mission Planner. If they are not the same, this error will happen. To match them, open your Mission Planner, connect it via telemetry, go to the **Advanced Parameter List**, and change HS1_TRIM and HS2_TRIM. With the roll and pitch stick cantered, the RC1 channel and RC2 channel should be the same as the values you wrote for the HS1_TRIM and HS2_TRIM parameters.

If the values are different, then calibrate your radio. The HS1 trim value must match the live stick cantered roll value, and the HS2 trim value must match the pitch stick cantered value. You must not use the radio trim for yaw. Make sure the center of gravity of the copter is dead center.

When I pitch or roll, the drone yaws

This can happen for several reasons. For the brushless AC motors, you need to swap any two of the three wires connected to the ESC. This will change the motor spinning direction. For the brushless DC motors, you need to check if the propellers are mounted properly, because the brushless DC motors do not move in the wrong directions unless the connection is faulty. Also, check that the drone's booms are not twisted. Calibrating the compass and magnetometer will also help if there is no hardware problem.

GPS lost communication

This happens because of a bad GPS signal. You can do one thing before launching the drone. You need to find a spot where the GPS signal is strong, so that it can be set to return to home or return to launch if the radio communication is lost. Before flying the drone, you may disarm the drone for a couple of minutes in a strong GPS signal.

Radio system failed

To solve this issue, we can use the radio amplifier. Using the radio amplifier can increase the signal strength. You can have radio failure when there is a minor block in between the drone and the receiver.

Battery life is too short

When, drone is not used, we should keep the battery stored at room temperature with low humidity. High temperature and moisture will cause the battery to damage the chemical elements inside the battery cells. This will result in a shorter battery life. For the LiPo battery, I would suggest using a balance charger.

Diagnosing problems using logs

For our ArduPilot, we used telemetry to communicate the drone to our Mission Planner. So, after the flight, we can analyze the telemetry logs. The telemetry logs are known as tlogs. There is Sik radio telemetry, Bluetooth telemetry, XBee, and so on. Before going any further, let's see where we can find the data files and how we can download them:

1. In the home screen, you will find the telemetry logs below the **Flight Data** panel. From there you can choose the graph type after loading the log.

2. When you load the logs, you will be redirected to a folder where the tlogs are situated. Click any of them to load. You can sort them by time so that you can be sure which data or log you need to analyze. You can also export your tlog data to a KML file for further analysis.

You can also see the 3D data of the flight path from the tlog files:

1. Open the Mission Planner's flight data screen. Click on the **Telemetry Log** tab and click on the button marked **Tlog>KML or Graph**. A new window will appear. Click on the **Create KML + GPX** button. A `.kmz` and `.kml` file will be created where the `.tlog` files are saved. In Google Earth, just drag and drop the `.kmz` file and you will see the 3D flight path.

2. You can see the graphs of the tlog files by clicking **Graph Log** on the screen after the **Togl>KMs or Graph** button has been clicked. From there you need to select the flight tlog and a **Graph this** screen will appear. Check the necessary data from the screen and you will see the graphs.

You can analyze the graphs depending on the data and troubleshoot your flight problems.

Radio control calibration problem

For the ArduPilot, the default channel mappings are as follow:

- **Channel 1**: Roll
- **Channel 2**: Pitch
- **Channel 3**: Throttle
- **Channel 4**: Yaw
- **Channel 5**: Flight modes
- **Channel 6**: Optional; it can do multiple things

To start the radio calibration, you need to remove the propellers from the drone and connect the ArduPilot via USB to the computer. Then turn on the RC transmitter. Your receiver will display a solid green light if the transmitter is bound to the receiver.

Fire up the Mission Planner and go to **Initial Setup | Mandatory Hardware | Radio Calibration**. Now, if you move the gimbals and knobs of the RC receiver, you can see the green bars moving. To start calibration, click the **Calibrate Radio** button and hit **OK**.

You need to move the control sticks (the gimbals we control using our thumbs) and toggle all the buttons and turn on and off the knobs to the maximum and minimum values. If you see the direction of the green bars move opposite, you need to change the setting for the channel-reverse-function from your remote. After the calibration is done, click on the **Click when Done** button and you will be shown a list of the channels with their highest values and their lowest values.

Now you need to turn off the radio and remove the battery to finish the calibration properly.

I would suggest that you do such calibrations after a few successful flights, as they may change depending on the flight path and type.

Summary

This was the last chapter of our book. I hope you have learned something about making a drone using Arduino, ESP8266, and other modules. The thing is, you can build drones by yourself if you just keep practicing. This book will not only inspire you to build something awesome, but all you need to make something that was never produced before. Just think of a kind of drone that has not been invented yet. Gather your idea and start building it. I hope you will be amused if you can do that. In this book, we have learned to build a number of drones. You can build them at home without any problems. This book is just a start to the journey of making basic drones and having ideas of the sensors that can be used in a drone. My suggestion is to play with sensors and IoTs so that you can later integrate them into your drone and, who knows, your drone might be a revolution. In this book, we have looked at tweaking the ESP8266 module and discussed the ArduPilot's drone. Basically, you can choose any flight controller and modify it. And the ESP8266 will help you to use the power of wireless technology. If you have any problems, just let me know. I will help you. Happy drone flying.

Other Books You May Enjoy

If you enjoyed this book, you may be interested in these other books by Packt:

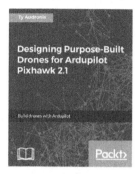

Designing Purpose-Built Drones for Ardupilot Pixhawk 2.1
Ty Audronis

ISBN: 978-1-78646-916-8

- Kitbash "dumb" objects into smart ones
- Program Pixhawk for your drones
- Fabricate your own parts out of different materials
- Integrate Pixhawk into different types of drones
- Build and understand the significant difference between land, sea, and air drones
- Adapt old Pixhawk sensors to the new Pixhawk 2.1 plugs
- Become familiar with procedures for testing your new drones

Raspberry Pi 3 Home Automation Projects
Shantanu Bhadoria, Ruben Oliva Ramos

ISBN: 978-1-78328-387-3

- Integrate different embedded microcontrollers and development boards like Arduino, ESP8266, Particle Photon and Raspberry Pi 3, creating real life solutions for day to day tasks and home automation
- Create your own magic mirror that lights up with useful information as you walk up to it
- Create a system that intelligently decides when to water your garden and then goes ahead and waters it for you
- Use the Wi-fi enabled Adafruit ESP8266 Huzzah to create your own networked festive display lights
- Create a simple machine learning application and build a parking automation system using Raspberry Pi
- Learn how to work with AWS cloud services and connect your home automation to the cloud
- Learn how to work with Windows IoT in Raspberry Pi 3 and build your own Windows IoT Face Recognition door locking system

Leave a review - let other readers know what you think

Please share your thoughts on this book with others by leaving a review on the site that you bought it from. If you purchased the book from Amazon, please leave us an honest review on this book's Amazon page. This is vital so that other potential readers can see and use your unbiased opinion to make purchasing decisions, we can understand what our customers think about our products, and our authors can see your feedback on the title that they have worked with Packt to create. It will only take a few minutes of your time, but is valuable to other potential customers, our authors, and Packt. Thank you!

Index

U

Made in the USA
Monee, IL
14 May 2020